Latin America
and the World

Latin America and the World

Leopoldo Zea

Translated from the Spanish by
Frances K. Hendricks and Beatrice Berler

With an Introduction by María del Carmen Millán

University of Oklahoma Press : Norman

By Leopoldo Zea

El Positivisimo en México (Mexico City, 1943)
Dos Etapas del Pensamiento en Hispanoamérica (Mexico City, 1949)
América en la Historia (Mexico City, 1957)
Latinoamérica y el Mundo (Caracas, 1960)
Democracias y Dictaduras en Latinoamérica (Mérida, 1960)
The Latin-American Mind (Tr. of *Dos Etapas del Pensamiento en Hispanoamérica* by James H. Abbott and Lowell Dunham, Norman, 1963)
América Latina y el Mundo (Buenos Aires, 1965)
Latin America and the World (Tr. of *América Latina y el Mundo* by Frances K. Hendricks and Beatrice Berler, Norman, 1969)

Library of Congress Catalog Card Number: 69–16718

María del Carmen Millán's Introduction

THE POINT OF DEPARTURE in examining the place of Leopoldo Zea in Latin American thought, as well as that of others who are inquiring into the attitude of the Latin American toward his world and facing his own reality, is undoubtedly *The Profile of Man and Culture in Mexico,* by Samuel Ramos (1897–1959). In a prologue to the third edition (1951) of this work, the author, in answering certain commentaries made since the appearance of the book in 1934, defined his work as an "essay of cultural analysis and philosophy" which attempts, through an interpretation of our history and the discovery of the more obvious national defects, "seriously to undertake a spiritual reform of Mexico." The book, in short, has a fundamentally moral character. In order to pursue his analysis rigorously, Ramos employed the tools of philosophy, history, and psychology. He was relentless in seeking out and examining cultural deficiencies, for he held that only awareness of these would make it possible to overcome them.

Confronted by a definite task, Ramos the philosopher put into practice his idea that

> Philosophy for us Spanish Americans is valuable not merely as a concept of the world and of human existence but also as an instrument for understanding our world and our life and our position in the general environment.

We want to see that world revealed by European philosophy, but we want to see it through American eyes, and we want to determine our own destinies in relation to the entire world.[1]

Ramos selected the *pelado* as the object of his examination. The *pelado*, with profoundly indigenous roots, represents a destitute social class; "economically, he ranks below the proletarian; intellectually, he is considered a primitive." This rather picturesque individual, mercilessly exploited by artists and writers, is studied here together with his responses, the determinants of his character, his fictitious personality, his apparent valor, his exalted sense of patriotism, and his masculine vanity. The psychological doctrine of Felix Adler, disciple of Freud, concerning the "virile protest," explains *machismo* as an unconscious compensation for an inferiority complex. From this doctrine Ramos derived some aspects of the Mexican's personality, such as his lack of confidence, his aggressiveness, and his extreme sensitivity. Through well-defined characteristics, the bourgeoisie manifest this same feeling of inferiority—that is, they use the means afforded by their position for perfecting a screen of dissimulation in order to escape from themselves and to live by an image of truth instead of by truth itself.

Another aspect of mestizo psychology, and a defense mechanism against the feeling of inferiority which Ramos considered responsible for Mexico's cultural failures, is the prevalence of imitation, which is as dominant in public life as it is in private. Ramos' thesis was developed with reference to the historical processes of the country. Within that framework, it explains the conflicts that Mexico has had to resolve in order to overcome its deficiencies and to carry forward its political and social reforms.

[1] *Historia de la filosofía mexicana* (Mexico City, 1943), 86.

This acute analysis of Mexican and Latin American culture effectively demonstrated many of the reasons for its peculiar character. Reversing the usual order, Ramos gave to his conclusions the validity necessary for undertaking the spiritual reform that had motivated him from the beginning.

The Profile of Man and Culture in Mexico, originally published in 1934 and reprinted several times, has stimulated some of those literary works of the past thirty years that have received the most attention and have most often been translated into other languages. *The Gesticulator*, written in 1938 by the dramatist Rodolfo Usigli, virtually gave birth to the Mexican theater, and was, in the words of its author, intended to combat falsehood and to propagate truth. The play's protagonist moves within a tragic world of imposture, becomes entangled in his own prevarications, and finally, under the pressure of circumstances, comes to live his own lie. Some of Alfonso Reyes' essays from 1936 also demonstrate this concern with Latin America's situation within Western culture.

Years later, in 1950, Octavio Paz published *The Labyrinth of Solitude*, which appeared at a time when the Hyperion group, of which Zea is a leader, had reached a peak of activity in its studies of Mexico and Mexicanism, offering a somewhat novel concept of the Mexican scene. With daring, clarity and penetration, Paz developed the themes first introduced by Ramos sixteen years earlier. Although there are many who lament Paz's lack of discipline, the book's undeniable brilliance assures it a large audience and continues to capture the attention of novelists, essayists, and philosophers who first lose and then find themselves in the labyrinth Paz sets before them. The Mexican's resentment, subterfuges, *machismo*, false nationalism, cultural

vii

uprooting, myths, and denial of the future are presented as various facets of a single phenomenon. Paz exhibits their true sources and hidden causes, in the process unintentionally supplying fruitful themes for contemporary writers, as, for example, the novelist, Carlos Fuentes.

Independent of the German phenomenologist school and of the Spaniard José Ortega y Gasset, Ramos followed a line traced earlier by other Mexican intellectuals. Concerned with both the present and the future of his country, his predecessors had applied themselves to an interpretation of history and were in some ways the spiritual leaders of that illustrious minority at the beginning of the century. Justo Sierra, minister of public education, re-established the National University in 1910, determined its course, and organized the public school system. He also interpreted the country's past in his *Political Evolution of the Mexican People.*

Not far removed from Justo Sierra were the young intellectuals of the Ateneo de la Juventud who destroyed inefficient systems set up by the reigning positivism of the era of Porfirio Díaz and who were the vanguard of the cultural revolution that was a part of the great social and political movements of those years. Among the youthful members of the Ateneo who tried, in the words of Ramos, to replace Bohemia with a cultural discipline by pursuing a moral ideal, three had special influence on succeeding generations: Antonio Caso, José Vasconcelos, and Alfonso Reyes. In spite of the climate of tragedy in which the group operated and which decided its inevitable dispersion, the lessons of the young masters produced results. Recognizing the debacle of positivism, Antonio Caso called for a return to the life of the spirit and claimed for philosophy the place that "scientific education," powerless to resolve the country's problems, had once occupied. Caso fought positivism from the classroom and from the pages of his books and articles, showing at the same time the new directions of contemporary thought, especially that culminating in Emile Boutroux, William James, and Henri Bergson.

The director of public education in the 1920's was the fiery José Vasconcelos, a gifted and restless spirit who launched daring, long-range projects and enlisted the aid of all artists, writers, and intellectuals who could raise the country's cultural level. His vitalist philosophy was oriented toward Latin America in search of a *raza cósmica*. Always a visionary, Vasconcelos discovered Latin America's possibilities as the land of the future.

Alfonso Reyes, who lived many years abroad, refined his remarkable literary talents in the Institute of Historical Studies in Madrid. His cultural interests were broadened by his wide reading, his travels, and his diplomatic duties. Supported by a vast and various literary production of remarkably high quality, Reyes became Mexico's most representative writer. Although Caso was accused—falsely—of devoting insufficient attention to national problems, it is difficult to find in Latin America's present generation of writers, anguished by the ills of their country, a theory or fact not previously considered by Reyes.

Samuel Ramos was the direct disciple of Caso and Vasconcelos. Dedicated, like his mentors, to philosophic investigations, he differed from them on some points but continued their method of studying Mexico's present situation in the light of its historical processes. By penetrating into the psychological aspect, Ramos made a considerable advance in this common area of study and offered more than a mere interesting theory. Ramos passed judgment on the Ateneo and found that its civilizing efforts did not reach the masses because the masses lacked the necessary cultural preparation. Ramos then dedicated himself to the study of man in Mexico, to the study of the *pelado* and of the bourgeoisie—the principal elements of urban population since the Revolution of 1910. His conclusions, as we have already stated, were aimed at helping raise the level of these groups, at making them conscious of their defects and hence more able to correct them.

Ramos believed that his study of man as the center of his universe must focus on the Mexican. His "philosophy is not utopian but realistic; it is not a philosophy of the future, but of the present; it does not tell us what we ought to be, or what destiny says we must be, but rather what we really are."[2]

Since the 1940's the philosophical panorama has broadened considerably in Latin America. It can now be said that all currents of European thought have their representatives there, whether foreigners or nationals. It is only logical, then, that the new generation of Mexican intellectuals have begun their investigations from much firmer, more eclectic bases. In these conditions, Leopoldo Zea, disciple of Ramos, proposes a "philosophy of Mexicanism."

Zea has devoted more than twenty years of scholarship to the theme of the Latin American's situation and circumstances in the world. He explains their great conflicts, such as the Mexican's struggle for recognition of his right to universality, his search for his origins, for his transcendency and his humanity which, according to Paz, must finally be found in "open solitude," behind the collapse of all values, where "nakedness and defenselessness await us . . . . We are

[2] Abelardo Villegas, *La filosofía de lo mexicano* (Mexico City, 1960), 119.

for the first time in our history the contemporaries of all men."

Coalescing around Zea in his adventurous search for our essential being, the Hyperion (child of the earth and the heavens, the concrete and the universal) circle of intellectuals tried, with the instruments of modern European philosophy, to approach impartially the theme of Mexicanism. This group, concentrating on circumstances common to all human beings and not belonging exclusively to the Mexican, has thrown new light on several old problems. "Mexicanism in itself cannot be a legitimate goal but only a point of departure, a means toward a broader and more responsible task."[3]

The Hyperion group understands Latin American philosophy in much the same way: it is false if it does not transcend its particular circumstances and dedicate itself to all that is human. The intellectual efforts of Latin America represent an attempt to assure itself of the human quality that the Western world has so far denied it.

Before Latin American intellectual studies were extensively taught and discussed in European and North American universities, they were being formally studied in 1943–44 in the Colegio de México. Results of the school's various seminars were published in *Jornadas*, an organ of its Social Studies Center. This publication, to use its own words, was concerned with "human matters considered in specifically American circumstantialities and those of our problems which require a theoretical consideration and a practical solution." José Gaos directed the seminar on Latin American thought and signed a special report on this subject.

[3] Leopoldo Zea, *Conciencia y posibilidad del Mexicano* (Mexico City, 1952), 23.

xi

Alfonso Caso, Augustín Yáñez, Mariano Picón Salas, Juan David García Bacca, and others participated in the discussions. Leopoldo Zea, then studying under a grant from the Colegio de México, had passed judgment on Mexican positivism (1943) and had demonstrated—as had his professors, Caso, Ramos, and Gaos—a capacity for investigations into our historical circumstances considered as the products of human experience.

In the realm of philosophy, concern for Latin America has found in Zea a most conscientious and faithful student. That same vitalist concept which moved his predecessors has carried Zea on an unbroken line into many areas of investigation, always with happy results. In his books, in his articles, and in his classes, Zea attempts to create a conscience in the Mexican and Latin American in order that the individual may find his own solutions and accept his responsibilities to the world in general. Zea understands, for example, that the internal struggles which marked Mexico from the War of Independence to the Revolution were only skirmishes in a greater struggle whose objective is the right to universality—Mexico's right to equality before the world, its right to decide its own destiny.

Zea has tried to eradicate those false perspectives which historical circumstances have given to Mexico, as well as to the rest of Latin America. Essentially, these result from that pathetic concept of "universality" put into circulation by advocates of European culture who consider extraneous all cultural manifestations which do not originate in Western Europe.

Arnold Toynbee, in *Mexico and the West*, has studied the reactions of a world dominated economically and spiritually by the West precisely in that moment in which, he believes, this domination is beginning to decline. If what

Toynbee says is true, that the tide is changing, then the peoples dominated by the West are responding to the challenge with means given them by the West itself—the free expression of their ideas. These ideas—and here Zea supports Toynbee—can now be discussed by Latin Americans in full awareness of their origins, and their points of view can then be used to resolve problems common to all mankind. For it must not be forgotten, as Zea insists, that the contributions of peoples considered to be on the margin of European culture to the universal search for man's essential being are also valid, and that these peoples represent a considerable share of the interests of the world.

Zea's contributions to the history of ideas has particular significance for Latin American culture. Indeed, the Latin American theme is the marrow of the main body of his writings. His travels through Europe, Asia, Africa, and North and South America have put him in contact with the most diverse realities and with other specialists dedicated, as he is, to investigating the evolution of the so-called underdeveloped countries in relation to their own circumstances and to the Western world. The publication, both here and abroad, of more than twenty-five books and many articles dealing with these matters, the translation of many of these books into other languages, together with his participation in international assemblies and congresses, give Leopoldo Zea a prominent place among contemporary Latin American intellectuals.

The present book, translated for the first time into English, presents a synthesis of the principal ideas which Zea has developed in other works. In *Latin America and the World*, Zea brings these ideas up to date and presents Mexico as an integral part of the Latin American community, sharing a common destiny and a particular culture

xiii

with a right to participate in solving the problems of the world of today. Beyond this, Mexico now reflects not only the Spanish American community of nations but also all other "third-world nations," such as those of Africa, Asia, and Oceania, who seek to apply their own solutions to their own problems.

Zea finds his point of departure in the results of World War II, in which the West, debasing its cultural values, offered the world a splendid example of barbarism. The new currents of philosophy suggest to Zea the necessity for creating a culture and for resolving its problems by the application of "personal, original creation." In other words, the European crisis has driven Latin America to seek its own paths and to demand its own right to universality. This enterprise must never depart from individual, human considerations. Latin America, conscious of its situation and linked by a common destiny, maintains itself in a state of readiness, alert to all the directions of modern thought. Whereas Europe once sought its future in America, despoiling and impoverishing it, today America is becoming conscious of its past and present and is facing up to Europe.

And the United States? If Latin America is a symbol of immaturity, the United States represents the full ripeness of the Western cultural inheritance. Latin America does not ignore or belittle the values of the United States, but it does oppose an attitude which apparently prohibits other nations from reaching the economic standards which the United States possesses and represents. Indonesia claims that it has not turned against the West, only against colonialism. India does not wish to break all its ties with England, but it does wish to maintain control of its own economy. Latin America, then, and the non-Western nations generally aspire to those values which should not be considered the exclusive property of one nation or bloc of nations. Zea explains how the cold war has been used as a means of reducing the Latin American countries to political and economic servitude, justified by the "so-called Communist threat and in the so-called interests of liberty and democracy."

One of the gravest problems that faces Latin America is that of landownership. Only after this problem is solved can the step to industrialization—which will presumably check the growing misery—be possible. The obstacles in the path to eventual industrialization can be traced, as is well known, to those nations which have already achieved a high level of industrialization.

Latin America's legitimate aspirations can perhaps be best realized through solidarity—an ideal solidarity made feasible by the common cultural origins of her peoples. Conscious of their situation in the world, they are now closer than ever before to that union of Latin America which had so fascinated—and eluded—the great liberators of these countries.

María del Carmen Millán

Mexico City
May 20, 1969

Contents

Latin America
and the World

Self-Discovery

I

As soon as the Latin American states achieved political independence, their main concern was to define the characteristics of their culture, which they found to be incompatible with that of such nations as England, France, and the United States, which had become leaders of modernity and progress. The newly founded states were soon aware that they were on the periphery of progress, on the periphery of the world rising vigorously beside them—indeed, even threatening them with its inevitable expansion. This concern had been expressed by the great liberator Simón Bolívar as well as by Domingo Sarmiento and Juan Alberdi of Argentina, Francisco Bilbao and José Lastarria of Chile, José Luis Mora of Mexico, and other great thinkers concerned with establishing order in the recently emancipated nations. In confrontation with the modern world the Latin American countries had to define the characteristics that would enable them to join or reject it as nations equally modern.

The political independence of the Latin American countries was actually a consequence of the concern aroused by their realization that they were outsiders to the modern world. European centers of Iberian culture also felt the impact of the so-called Western world. Problems arose there which would soon concern Latin America. The newly

3

independent countries assumed attitudes toward the mother countries derived from the modern world. They talked of sovereignty of the people, whereas the mother countries based everything on sovereignty derived from God. The pioneers of political emancipation of the Latin Americans certainly tried at first to reconcile the points of view of the colonial heritage with those of Modernity. They held that sovereignty of the people did not necessarily conflict with religion. Precisely on the basis of religion, however, the mother countries justified their sovereign rights over the colonies. These rights were, in one way or another, of divine origin. God himself had determined the subordination of peoples to their kings and rulers and that of the colonies to the mother country where those kings and rulers governed. People had to obey the will of their rulers as an expression of the divine will, which was superior to any particular human interest or to society in general. The old idea of Christian empire, which had motivated Spain and Portugal to expand throughout the world, continued to function, although without the impetus which made possible the empire on which the sun never set. Now this empire, far from expanding throughout the globe, was receding, shrinking, before the pressure of another empire—before the impact of the nations forming the world we now call Western.

Conciliation between Christianity and Modernity, possible in the sixteenth century and successfully expressed in ideas such as those of the Spanish Erasmians, was impossible now in the epoch in which the Latin American nations began their struggle for independence. Even before rising in open rebellion, these peoples had tried to reconcile the past which had fallen to their lot with the future they hoped to achieve. Consequently, before they recognized the necessity of choosing between the past and the future—between

4

what they had been and what they hoped to be—there emerged a body of doctrines which expressed the eagerness for conciliation and which became generally known by the significant name of "eclecticism." The impossibility of such a conciliation soon became apparent. Intransigence on the part of the mother countries provoked intransigence in the colonies, who chose the course of rebellion. Far from appearing to the new nations as a stimulus, as a step toward achieving the longed-for progress, the past seemed an obstacle. The new nations learned that they could enter the modern world, could travel the road to progress, only by renouncing a past which, far from serving the future, actually obstructed it. The new ideas were openly and violently contradictory to the spirit imposed on the colonies by the mother countries. The idea of civilization symbolized the future in contrast with a past which refused to be past and which opposed all change. "Civilization or barbarism!" was the dilemma Sarmiento posed. "Catholicism or republicanism!" cried Bilbao. One could not exist with the other; there had to be a choice. Conciliation was impossible.

Thus Latin America became prey to internal divisions. One part—the passive majority—chose the past; the other—an active minority which tried to arouse the others—chose the future. One group was determined to preserve the heritage of the past without alteration; the other was pledged to realize that future so brilliantly achieved by other peoples even though it meant throwing overboard all the heritage of the past. These internal struggles within the Latin American nations became so virulent that one faction threatened the total destruction of the other.

The progressive group, which chose to march toward the future even at the cost of absolute rejection of the past, found great examples to follow in the political, economic, social, and cultural institutions of such modern nations as England, the United States, and France. From these Western nations, they borrowed legislation, ideas, literature, art, and customs. In imitating, in feeling themselves more French, English, or Yankee, many Latin Americans ended, however, in feeling alien—men in exile within the reality which, whether they wished it or not, belonged to them. The Europeanized or Westernized men who shaped Latin American culture at the close of the nineteenth and beginning of the twentieth century came finally to feel themselves not only exiles from European or Western culture but outcasts from culture itself. They had no place in the reality characteristic of America; neither did they belong to a reality which they wished in vain to make their own. They were neither Americans nor Europeans; they did not wish to continue to be the former, and they could not be the latter. They became men hoping for a future wholly disengaged from the past in a present which was only an expectation.

In this situation developed the great preoccupation of Latin Americans with what constituted the distinctive nature of their own culture. Andrés Bello, Lastarria, Sarmiento, Alberdi, Mora, José de la Luz y Caballero, Juan Montalvo, and many other men of eminence in Latin American culture began to inquire into the nature and definition of that culture. These men raised questions about whether there existed a literature truly characteristic of Latin America. They wanted to know, along with Alberdi, who had already brought the matter into the open, whether there was an American philosophy. Even more generally, they inquired: is there an American culture? They felt that there must be something essentially Latin American in its nations and its men—something which defined them as such, which could be the point of departure for the realiza-

6

tion of what they aspired to be. They were unable to develop a concept of themselves within the emptiness of a past they did not accept or in the face of the emptiness of a future that did not—indeed, could not—exist. Even though they felt themselves outcasts from a culture not yet their own, exiles from a history they had not made, these nations and these men were, nevertheless, creating a history. Although it was of course not European history, it was certainly a part of it—perhaps a part, whether or not important, of Western history, or indeed, what was even more significant, a part of the history of man. In one way or another, in the course of creating a history these nations were producing a culture—that is, a set of values and principles, needing only to be made known, which necessarily expressed a mode of being, the distinctive experience of certain men in particular circumstances who had no reason to feel therefore that their experiences were inferior to those of other men.

A renewed concern with the matter of identity has been central to our times in Latin America. Questions concerning culture raised by thinkers of other days have been stated anew in the face of a world crisis in the culture that had in the past served as an inspiration to our forefathers. This cultural crisis has stripped our models of ready answers and left them in a situation similar to ours—that is, under the necessity of posing questions and seeking answers without being able to find them anywhere except in themselves. The consequence is that the search for identity apparently peculiar to our countries concerns also other nations of the world which seek to find and to know themselves in broader terms—in relationships to nations and men which would transcend existing narrow limits.

Men of other nations ask themselves, with the same anguish that racks us, what they have been, what they are,

7

and what they can become. Many now seek the same goals that we have sought. In Asia, Africa, the Middle East, and Oceania, nations are rising which, like ours, have reacted against the impact of the Western world and which now try to achieve for themselves much of what is worthwhile in that civilization. Men of these nations ask the question which our forefathers raised and which we are still asking: what is my place in the world of culture?

Just as we do, these nations insist on participating in tasks that are no longer regarded as belonging only to an elite group of nations but to all the peoples who comprise humanity. Nations like ours insist on universalizing Western culture and taking its best expressions as those of all human-kind and, therefore, of all men and all nations without regard to their special circumstances or situations.

From this point of view it is evident that Latin American nations were the forerunners of the efforts to westernize now occuring in Asia, Africa, Oceania, and the Middle East. In the same way that we did, countries in those areas, on feel-ing the impact of that culture, have turned it into something their own. Arnold Toynbee has already analyzed in depth the effort, still not understood by the Western world itself, that non-Western nations are making to universalize West-ern culture, an effort which Latin Americans were the first to attempt with an eagerness for Westernization of which they were well aware.

It is possible for us to say that this is where our America has been able to find itself and to provide an answer to the old and grievous questions concerning what it is and what it could become. We are no longer a collection of ill-defined countries suspended somewhere between reality and fantasy. We now discover that our goals are also those of many other nations of the world in a situation similar to ours. Consequently, statesmen and Latin American men of culture can now affirm that Latin America is creating universal history —it is sharing an endeavor with others whose conditions are similar to ours. Along with us, other nations are demanding the right to active participation in the creation and enjoyment of material and spiritual values not yet available to all who long to enjoy the fruits of modern science and technology. Thus, some quarter of a million Latin Americans struggle to achieve the same goals for which many millions in other parts of the world also strive. The Argentinian Arturo Frondizi said, "Our struggle is part of the world-wide struggle which at this moment is being carried on to dignify human beings both spiritually and materially."[1] It is in this struggle that Latin America has found itself and has acquired a truly genuine sense of a culture that has been in the process of creation throughout its inevitable history. The essential meaning of all culture is that which is human. To the insistent and continual questions about his existence and the future of his culture which the Latin American has propounded, one answer can now be given: the Latin American is only a man among other men, and his culture is the concrete expression of what is human—no more and no less.

Thus an experience which has seemed unique to us and, because of our absurd inferiority complex, worthless, turns out to be one shared by many other men and nations. Other people who had seemed to us exotic and foreign now show us that, in spite of many social and cultural differences, their problems are ours and our solutions can be theirs, or vice versa. By digging deep into ourselves, by rooting out a host of our own prejudices—masks that prevent us from recognizing ourselves in others and being recognized in turn—we

[1] *Petróleo y política* (Buenos Aires, 1954), lxxi.

9

will find the source of the genuine universality sought by all philosophers and presupposed by the most prestigious cultures: mankind. As to what concerns us, we Latin Americans have found in ourselves the universality that our forefathers sought so earnestly and which they tried to achieve by the easy but false road of imitation which appeared to them in the disguise of universality.

There is, however, more to this meeting with the Man who is the particular expression of each of us, although there may be a number of circumstantial differences which by their very existence also express human individuality. In this encounter we have, in the immediate past, chanced to meet men who boasted of representing mankind par excellence to the exclusion of any type other than what they represented. We find men who after two great wars are forced to recognize that one culture, one race, or one simple group does not exhaust the universality of humanity. This man (I refer to European and Western man in general) has arrived at the same understanding that we have concerning what is authentically human—a humanity which is not exhausted in any one culture, race, religion, or social situation. Through the crisis in the culture that has been considered the epitome of all culture, this man can grasp the limitations of his circumstances, common to all men, as well as the universality of the expressions of his culture when these latter refer to the values that can and should be recognized in other men—that can and should be attainable by any man regardless of the circumstances in which he may find himself.

Just as we have, the best representatives of the new Europe of our time have turned their eyes inward. Casting out prejudices and putting aside pretensions of superiority and presumptions of grandeur, they have begun to recognize themselves as brothers of other men, as similar to other men. Albert Camus, Jean-Paul Sartre, Simone Weil, Graham Greene, Albert Schweitzer, Arnold Toynbee, and others recognize in their limitations those of all men—hence the authentic universality of that which is human. In the suffering, anguish, and bitterness of destruction and death characteristic of the latest world war, the most eminent Western men became aware of the humanity of other men—black, bronze, yellow, green, and so on—who had for a long time suffered those same afflictions and had been treated as though they were subhuman. This group of Westerners has finally gained an insight into the depth of the expression of the humanity that is common to all men—to those who are citizens of great powers as well as to those of countries called, rather rudely, underdeveloped, to French and Algerians, to English, Arabs, and Hindus, to North Americans, Chinese, and Latin Americans.

Consequently, although for different reasons and by no less different ways, we and the men who served us in the immediate past as models, on turning in upon ourselves, have found and recognized ourselves simply as men and have put aside notions of inferiority or superiority. In this encounter, for the first time in our own history—now part of Western history—and in that of many other countries that formerly seemed alien to us, similarities appear which can bring us together in a future which belongs to us all. The Mexican poet Octavio Paz, in agreement with the European Camus, found it possible to say in his *El laberinto de la soledad*: "Nakedness and helplessness await us. Transcendence also awaits us there in the infinite solitude: the hands of others who are alone. We are for the first time in our history contemporaries of all men."[2]

[2] Third edition (Mexico City, 1959), 150.

"Contemporaries of all men"—the best expression of that longed-for universality sought in vain through feelings of superiority or through imitation, a universality already accorded us and which can continue by means other than those of solitude and suffering—that is, the way of solidarity in the attainment of a future that of necessity we have in common. As all men and all nations exert their efforts to achieve something as definite as the minimum of material and spiritual happiness to which all men are entitled without social, political, economic, or racial discrimination, they will create that solidarity.

We have met not only Europe and Europeans—the West and Westerners—on a footing of equality but also men of other countries who have lived or are now living in circumstances similar to our own. They face problems that have been and continue to be ours, among them the so-called problem of the Middle East, where Arab nations demand recognition of international rights which the colonizing nations had previously claimed for themselves. Arab nations have learned their nationalism from the West. There are many other expressions of nationalism, such as that of India, of Indonesia, or of the Negro countries of Africa. We are well acquainted with the sort of nationalism that now unfurls its banners. We raised such banners long ago in our extended struggle for independence.

That nationalism demands freedom, the right of self-determination, sovereignty. These are the same principles that have been upheld by the people from whom recognition is demanded—the Western nations themselves in their expansion over the earth. From this point of view we can no longer speak of exotic countries that are strange or foreign to us and to our principles and purposes. Leaders of Asiatic or African nationalism speak words we have already heard from the lips of our greatest leaders.

That nationalism had its origin in expressions of Western culture, but it now belongs to countries who are proclaiming it and are demanding it from its creators. It is decidedly different from the nationalism which the Western nations developed in expanding throughout the world; it is solely the expression of the rights of all countries to self-determination. It does not, however, imply an assumed right to trample over other peoples, but is, instead—purely and simply—the right of all countries to develop as nations among nations with all which that implies with respect to responsibilities to themselves and to others. This nationalism should depend more on a sense of international solidarity than on irresponsible individualism unmindful of all that does not conform to its own most particular interests. Nations proclaiming this nationalism cannot and do not aspire to a new partition of the world inasmuch as they themselves have already suffered such an unjust partition. According to this nationalism, progress and prosperity do not rest on the ruin and misery of others. This nationalism expresses its best aspects and dismisses those of a negative character. Sukarno, among others, has spoken insistently of this nationalism, which has had its origin in Latin America, Asia, Africa, and Oceania. He said, *"To understand Asia and Africa, we must understand nationalism."*

What, then, is nationalism? It is a Western idea but one adapted to the new nations and for which non-Western nations or those on the periphery of the Western world, such as the Latin American nations, have struggled for during many decades. According to Sukarno,

We, the Indonesians and the citizens of many countries in Asia and Africa have seen our dearest and best suffer and die, struggle and fail, and rise again to struggle and fail again—and again be resurrected from the very earth and finally achieve their goal. Something burned in them, something which inspired them. They called it national-ism. We who have followed and have seen what they built, but also what they destroyed themselves in build-ing, we, too, call their inspiration, and our inspiration as well, nationalism. For us there is nothing ignoble in that word. On the contrary it contains for us all that is best in mankind. . . .

Therefore I say, do not denigrate our nationalism. . . . It is at least a positive creed, an active belief, and has none of the cynicism and lassitude of less virile outlooks.[3]

The distinctive aspect of Latin American, Asiatic, and African nationalism is its opposition to the most negative aspect of Western nationalism: colonialism. The people of all these regions know that they should not depend on achieving greatness and prosperity by means of any forces or sacrifices other than their own. Other countries no longer appear on the horizon of history which could pay for our greatness and prosperity as we have paid for that of the Western nations. We can achieve our goals only by our own efforts and with no external support other than the feelings of a community of interests by which we can give and receive from other nations whose aims we share. There can be no more enforced contribution from the weak to the strong, no more of what Jawaharlal Nehru pointed out about India with respect to the sacrifices that the non-Western world had to make to produce the greatness and

[3] Address to the National Press Club, Washington, D.C., May 18, 1956. U.S. Department of State *Bulletin* XXXIV (June 4, 1956), 936.

prosperity of the West. "It may be said," the Hindu leader stated, "that a great part of the costs of transition to industrialism in Western Europe was paid by India, China, and the other colonial countries whose economy was dominated by European powers."[4] The so-called underdeveloped peoples paid with hunger and death for all the greatness and prosperity achieved by the West.

This is precisely what other peoples will be unable to do for us. Even though our sacrifices made possible the greatness of foreign nations, we cannot ask others to do the same for us. The most discerning men in the present-day Western cultures are also coming to this conclusion. They are trying to effect changes in a political system which is anachronistic in a world that, if it is to continue to exist, must do so by means of collaboration, by a just sharing of sacrifices and benefits. Indeed, only by coordination, by the unification of many interests that have divided the world and have provoked the injustices subsequently paid for by terror and death, will survival be possible in a world which is ever more bound together by its interests and which will otherwise easily become explosive.

Such is the world we Latin Americans have encountered in our insistent search for identity and for the destiny of our countries. What formerly seemed distinctive—even shameful—about us is but the expression of a situation now apparent in many parts of the world. In the twentieth century of marvelous mechanical wonders—atomic devices, satellites, lunar missiles, and other extraordinary inventions of men—the world has been made much smaller and consequently better known. It has been, and will continue to be, the fullness of our possibilities, which now transcend the terrestrial sphere and are directed toward infinite space,

[4] *The Discovery of India* (New York, 1956), 300.

15

which permits us to attain that minimum of human solidarity so necessary for ending a multitude of injustices.

At this point we Latin Americans are discovering ourselves. We find that we are not a special people, original or singular, but one similar to all other peoples of the world. We are neither inferior nor superior to other men or nations, but like them and, on that account, have the same possibilities and natural limitations that circumstances create. Such an awareness will enable us, as it does others, to achieve that community of interests that seemed to have disappeared from a world being ruled in accordance with the inhuman utilitarian and positivist principles of a supposed struggle for existence in which only the strong could triumph.

The new solidarity which shows promise of being realized will have to be distinct from the circumstantial material success which does not inspire the highest values in Man—in the particular man, man here and now, and the one on whom the future depends, in the man to whom it is also essential that he be from some given place or another, to have one special kind of skin or another, one religion or another, one set of opinions or another, but without on that account being any less a man. For coming to grips with this world in which we Latin Americans have found ourselves, few find themselves as well endowed as we are.

The Latin American Experience

II

As EARLY AS 1954, both UNESCO and the European Society of Culture, with its headquarters in Venice, undertook studies and held conferences concerning the relations of the culture of the Old World with that of the New. Even though Latin America participated in these studies and conferences, it occupied a somewhat secondary place in European attention, for America continued to be purely and simply the United States. Distinguished figures of European culture still viewed that country as the symbol of youthful rebellion and, because it was youthful, as immature. That rebellion and immaturity appeared menacing to the old European culture of which America was the daughter. Much was said in these conferences about Hollywood, jazz, and other manifestations considered characteristic of North American culture which, along with Coca-Cola, had been invading the pre-eminent centers of European culture.

At one of these conferences, held in São Paulo, Brazil, in 1954, Latin Americans were able to make a stronger impression in presenting to European delegates problems which had previously escaped their attention. Here was the other America, previously ignored, calling attention to its problems not only in relation to the European world and its culture but also in relation to the other America. Somewhat unexpectedly, Latin America was bringing her experiences to bear in an area new to Europeans. Europe itself was beginning to feel pressures of a kind which Latin America had suffered in the recent past. The source of these pressures was a new American nation which was being held up as Europe's most legitimate heir.

Europeans were beginning to raise their voices against just these political and economic pressures, fearing the fragmenting effect of this menace, which would destroy the values of the old universal culture. The great empires of Western Europe had shrunk little by little and had suffered in turn the strong influence of the new imperialism born in North America. The old Western empires not only suffered loss of their colonies but were themselves converted into new colonies. Europe was no longer the center of the world, the cultural, economic, and political axis of humanity, but instead had become a collection of minor pieces in a game manipulated by new powers which only yesterday had figured secondarily in the universal history created by Western nations. On one side was Russia; on the other, the United States. If the first seemed menacing for the future of Western culture, then the other seeemd no less so. Certainly the United States was not, nor did it pretend to be, more than the expression and development of the culture that had originated in Europe. Nevertheless it was oriented along paths which no longer were—nor could be—those which Western Europe would have followed had it been in control.

Displaced from the center of the world economically and politically, Western Europe accommodated itself to the situation by maintaining a supposed cultural primacy bestowed on it by having been the cradle of the great expressions of that culture. Europeans defended that claim to

18

primacy when specific problems of relations of the Old World with the New were raised. Old values of Western culture were put on the defensive against the presumed intention of North America to assume a claim to primacy.

In these defensive efforts, Latin America, which counted for little in that connection, was forgotten. Also forgotten were her experiences that were similar to those now current in relations between Western Europe and the United States. Forgotten was the America which was heir to a tradition which had made possible much that was worthwhile in Modernity. Forgotten was the America which, since the beginning of her liberty, since her undertaking the task of becoming a family of nations, had clashed with the America of manifest destiny. Forgotten was the America which had struggled to contain the impetus of a destiny alien to it. This was the America whose highest expressions were epitomized in a Bolívar confronting the America expressed in a Monroe. Although the European representatives at the above-mentioned conferences practically ignored this America, it had already passed through experiences that could have provided Europe with insight into the experiences she was suffering for the first time in her history.

The North American representatives, more sagacious than their European colleagues, immediately sensed the dual opposition—of Europe and of Latin America—to North American expansion in the world. With the greatest candor and innocence, they asked for an explanation of this opposition. After all, North America had been a good daughter of Europe; she had been most faithful in carrying on the traditions of Europe, and had used her forces in two world wars against Prussian imperialism and totalitarianism to save from possible extinction a culture that was also her own. In a critical time the United States had been aware of the necessity of aiding that culture in the face of danger and of helping it restore itself.

On the other hand, the United States had presented a prime example for her sister republics of Latin America to follow. North American political and economic institutions served as models as the Latin American republics attempted to reorganize in accord with the times. George N. Shuster spoke to his numerous European and Latin American listeners of how much the United States had done to be both a good daughter and a good sister.[1] The North American, he said, has shown the world how to profit by technology and how it can be put to the service of man. Thanks to technology and its utilization, North America has provided a society in which its "children enjoy a larger measure of security, perhaps, than young people have ever known." Also as a consequence of this technological advantage, women of North America "can be emanicipated from grueling physical labor." Another result is the bountiful production of the fruits of the earth. At the same time that population has increased, resources for its sustenance and security have been augmented. Medicine has conquered numerous epidemic diseases which would otherwise have decimated the population. In general the people are conscious of the "ability to establish a social order, which despite the need for improvement and for modification in detail, is fundamentally satisfying to the vast majority of those who live in it." This "is a reason for pride. . . . It may be concluded that the American is . . . inclined to consider the outlook for progress in all that might conceivably affect

[1] "Cultural Relations between the Old World and the New," address delivered in São Paulo, August, 1954. (Department of State, United States National Commission for UNESCO. Washington, D.C., n.d.). All quotations from the address are from this pamphlet, 7, 15, 17.

the mundane lot of man as being very good indeed." Nevertheless, he added, we are attacked, we are misunderstood.

> Perhaps, one may say . . . that what is particularly tragic about the present world situation, so heartrendingly ominous in nearly every sense, is this—while unprecedented American technological achievement has made possible the discovery of weapons of destruction which, if employed, might well render the continued existence of the human race impossible, general world-wide regard for the generosity, idealism and restraint of the American people has . . . reached a low ebb.

This forlorn declaration anticipated later attitudes, such as that which made possible the nomination of the extremist candidate Barry Goldwater, who demanded a revindication of the prestige of the United States in the world even though this might mean the total destruction of that world. Various actions have revealed a lack of understanding by groups which feel themselves misunderstood on account of the fact that their material needs, not adapted to the world of progress, are limited or restricted. Far from diminishing their demands, however, they increase them and, in the process, propose systems and doctrines which the United States had long considered its exclusive possession.

Latin America can provide explanations for the misunderstanding with which it has been charged. Latin America, as well as parts of the non-Western world, has always been aware of, and has admired and acknowledged, the extraordinary contribution of North America to the progress of all peoples—the best example of technology put to the use of man. Latin Americans, as well as Asiatics and Africans, long to live in a social order full of security and without restrictions on the highest expressions of human

21

freedom. They also long to live in a world in which women can be freed not only from domestic work but from the hard work they are forced to endure in those regions where colonization endeavors to exploit to the maximum nature and human beings who make possible that exploitation. Like North Americans, they long for a world in which epidemics disappear and everyone can enjoy the boon of good health, for a world in which men who work receive the fruits of their labor, and for a world in which the increase of population, far from being a misfortune, is instead a stimulant for development and for the attainment of greatness.

Latin Americans admire all this in a nation which has been able to achieve it as they admire the idealism, the generosity, and the restraint which have made it possible. But because they admire that example and because they try to follow it in their own countries, they challenge and struggle against any who oppose them in the attainment of their goals and against all the obstacles in their way. In this, they do neither more nor less than the country which is the model has done in achieving its success. They are struggling, on the one hand, against the opposition of internal forces which refuse to countenance a transformation that would imply the end of their privileges and, on the other hand, against external forces which, though models of what any truly human order ought to be, refuse to admit the realization of these goals in any country but their own. Yet, in spite of all that is said, much of the greatness for which they are anxious, depends on the sacrifices of some groups for the benefit of others.

Our peoples wish nothing that other nations, such as the United States, which continues to serve as an example, do not wish for themselves. Consequently, Latin Americans are surprised and irritated when they encounter hostility instead of help in their efforts to emulate the model. The Brazilian Paulo Duarte said at that memorable conference in São Paulo that few men have had the distressing experience "of the free men of Latin America who, being oppressed by one of the several forms of Latin American fascism, have seen and still see these false and arbitrary rulers recognized and honored by the United States even while they engage in their cruel work of suppressing individual liberty—the liberty of free men—in this part of America."[2]

There is, then, no such underrating or lack of understanding of the best qualities of North America; even less is there that superiority which Europeans are assumed to feel over North Americans. On the contrary, there is the most lively desire to attain the kinds of benefits which the United States enjoys even in the face of obstacles put in the way of that attainment by the interests of those who created the obstacles—that is, the United States. Moreover, the fruits of that culture, like those of all Western culture, are claimed as a universal patrimony by those peoples who have become aware of their own undeniable humanity.

Shortly after the meeting in São Paulo, the United States experienced the distressing incidents of Vice-President Richard Nixon's tour of Latin America. What happened brought to the fore the often suppressed problem of the relations between the two Americas. That problem has indirectly affected the relations of the United States with other countries in a situation similar to ours, as in the countries in Asia and Africa where a "vacuum" appeared in the economic and political influence of the West as soon as the nations of Western Europe withdrew from those

[2] *El viejo y el nuevo mundo* (Paris, 1956), 19.

areas where they had formerly maintained their predominance. Experiences gained by the United States in relations with Latin America would be valuable in the former's relations with other countries, including Europe itself, and also in relations between countries different from the very time of their origin, each having its own vision of the world and of life which seemed not only opposed but actually antagonistic to the others. This diversity of visions concerns a world that still poses unresolved problems, such as those raised by nations in Africa and Asia which the United States encounters in her expansion in the world. The experience of the United States has made even more difficult relations with a Europe which, such as the one Charles de Gaulle endeavors to lead, seeks to be independent of the predominance of the United States without falling into the other sphere of influence which opposes it. That Europe, having lost its world-wide predominance, now seeks to preserve itself as an independent force and tries, in addition, to develop closer relations with the countries of Asia, Africa, and Latin America. It offers these countries help, which enables them, in turn, to be an important part of a world not yet resigned to being merely the instrument of interests alien to them.

The world can derive benefit from our experiences with the United States—experiences which can no longer continue being regarded in the simplistic manner which has been a product of the cold war. The problems arising from these relations is much older than those that now characterize the conflict in which the United States and the U. S. S. R. are engaged in their eagerness to expand over the rest of the world. This problem cannot be resolved with references to the supposed struggle between the so-called free world and the socialist world. This is an old problem, originating in the free world and a consequence of it, and one which must be resolved if there is a real desire to strengthen the whole world. It is a problem that can only incidentally, and in favor of alien interests, be narrowed down to antagonism between liberalism and socialism. We have already noted that the source of the problem is the awareness that countries like ours have their own capacities for achieving social, political, and economic values which the United States has claimed solely for herself.

A long time before our world was divided into two zones of expansion by the two ideologies now demonstrating their antagonisms, problems arose in Latin America that are not only still unresolved but are actually complicated by the conflict in which the two great powers of the contemporary world are locked. These problems, involving Christian and Western peoples of the same European origins who have pursued diverse lines of development on their transfer to America, could have been resolved with a modicum of knowledge, with a spirit of understanding. These problems have arisen from the encounter between the Anglo-Saxon America, disposed to achieve in the new lands its ideal of liberal humanism, and the Iberian America, determined to maintain the old ideals of Christian community, the heritage of its forefathers. These points of view now produce in Europe itself, where they originated, a critical conflict between the Iberian world and the rest of Western Europe. The development of two Americas, diverse in their political, economic, social, and cultural development, is an expression of the clash.

The differences between the two Americas ultimately became a disadvantage both to Ibero-America and to Spain and Portugal. The United States, and with it the countries of Western Europe, became leaders in the progress to which

25

the New World was oriented. Latin American countries were the first to realize the disadvantage in which they stood in relation to the Western countries in a world in which the particular individual, subject to his own strengths and weaknesses, was the only responsible author of his future in a world in which the most apt and capable—the strongest and most cultured—commanded respect. From the moment Latin Americans became aware of the situation, they felt themselves at a great disadvantage in comparison with their neighbors in America and their counterparts in Europe. The situation produced the great reaction that the leaders of Latin American emanicipation and reform experienced against their own cultural roots. For the evils and disadvantages in a world they had not made, they blamed their past, blamed Spain and Portugal, blamed even their belonging to one race rather than another. The first reaction of our great leaders was to break with the past in which our countries had been formed.

Proponents of Modernity in Europe and America undertook of course to make their physical and cultural superiority felt in a world which they had created. They demonstrated this superiority by expanding into non-Western countries, including the Iberian and Latin American ones. For that expansion they found an easy justification in an ideology in which freedom, understood as free enterprise, provided the stimulus for the achievement of the invariable triumph of those considered the best and most capable among individuals and nations. Latin American nations and many of their best men have felt that this ideology placed them in an inferior position. It seemed to them that their social origins and cultural heritage had made them ineffective in a struggle in which the assumption was that those who succeeded were the ones who were capable and best prepared for the struggle. Consequently, on achieving political emancipation, these men were most anxious to attain what they considered intellectual or cultural emancipation from the Iberian mother countries. Bello, Sarmiento, Lastarria, Mora, Montalvo, and many others dedicated themselves to this goal. In order to achieve complete political emancipation, Latin Americans should become capable of engaging in the struggle and of triumphing in the world created by the new Western states. They must extirpate a heritage which prevented their even entering into collaboration with such leading nations as England, France, and the United States—much less into full competition.

In these circumstances, few nations have admired the United States as those of Latin America have. A nation arose in the northern part of America which served as a model and a stimulus to the recently emancipated countries. "We may become the United States of South America," said various leaders of Latin America in their enthusiasm for achieving in their countries the ideals of liberty, democracy, and progress which they saw incarnated in the vigorous nation of the North. Unfortunately, these aspiring nations had to struggle not only with the obstacles of a past that resisted the abandonment of canonries and old prebends but also with the ever increasing interests of the members of the nations they wished to imitate. The eagerness for Westernization or Americanization ran headlong into a lack of comprehension and opposition of the nations that served as their models. Ibero-America, far from receiving the help it might have expected in its desire to emulate the United States and other Western nations, has been hindered by them in its endeavor to achieve betterment for itself. Consequently, a seeming contradiction appeared—a feeling of repudiation arose in the same men who had pointed out the road to follow. Although they never wavered in their profound admiration for Washington, Lincoln, Roosevelt, and Kennedy, they repudiated the North America that expanded its territory at the expense of Mexico in 1847, Panama in 1903, and other places in the Americas at various times. They repudiated the North America of Manifest Destiny which ignored the interests of any other country.

The shape that relations between Latin America and the United States will inevitably take is appearing above the horizon. On one side is the North America admired by Latin American nations endeavoring to achieve their greatest worth; on the other is the North America repudiated by those same nations who have seen it scheming with forces representative of a past unresigned to being past. On the one side is admiration for the North America that stands for freedom; on the other is repudiation for the North America that incites and supports those who impede freedom in Latin America. Both admiration and repudiation are henceforth going to characterize relations of the two. These attitudes are unrelated to the disputes arising between the United States and the U. S. S. R.; indeed, they are antecedent to them and independent of them. Problems in relations between Latin America and North America should be resolved with reference to circumstances uncomplicated by those ensuing from the cold war that followed World War II.

Thus the central problem of the relations of the two Americas is connected with the effort to achieve the values to which the Western world adheres. Must their realization be limited to individuals and countries that are Western? Rather, should it not be possible for all men, without any discrimination, to realize them? Difficulties between the

28

two Americas and, in general, between the Western and non-Western worlds are not, as in the past, matters of the displacement of one culture by another. Latin America has no desire to impose its point of view and values on the United States and on other nations; neither does the non-Western world wish to do so. On the contrary, the objective is the creation in Latin America, or in all the non-Western world, values regarded as not belonging exclusively to a given country or group of countries.

The problem is no longer that of the past ranged against the future; it is not a repetition of Spain's struggle against Modernity, represented by Western Europe. It is not a question of reinstating a past already considered finished. After an extended struggle, our countries have resolved the problem of a past which resisted displacement. Now the problem is the West's opposition, with a force greater than that of the conquered past, to the entrance of other countries into its world. The West resists what we would call the universalization of the culture it represents. This, the great problem of our day, is the source of misunderstanding between Latin America and the United States; between nations recently emancipated from the political tutelage of Western countries and those same Western countries. The new countries of Asia and Africa have come into existence struggling for what we Latin Americans sought—that is, the adoption and realization of the great principles of liberty and democracy upheld by Western culture as well as the adoption of techniques that have made possible the material progress of Western nations.

In recent years many nations have sought such goals. In this connection, the experience of Latin America can be useful not only for these new countries but also for a West better disposed to understand the world that has arisen from its action. The key to the problem lies in the fact that a world difficult to comprehend has arisen from the action and precepts of the West and is its legitimate heir. This world created by the West wants or claims nothing that the West itself has not attained. The antagonism between the two worlds is not a conflict of ideals but is the product of a lack of understanding by the one that has not kept pace with the results of its own actions. The world created by the West's action has transcended its very creators, who no longer seem to be on the same plane as their own creations because they continue viewing the world in relation to the narrow interests which motivated their action. Actually the language used to describe the demands of the new nations is anachronistic; those nations have given new meanings to old terms. Adjustments must be made for interests that can no longer maintain the pretensions of the past, in which Western peoples had the principal voice. This voice, still Western, belongs now also to peoples who feel themselves united in a task in which all nations and men can participate.

I am firmly convinced that our America can greatly assist this emerging world. Situated between two worlds—the West and the non-West—we continue our efforts to deal with conditions growing out of anxieties we have long experienced and now have in common with many countries. If the countries which provoked these anxieties by their expansion could understand them, then a more responsible and stable world would result. The nations that have learned the lessons of the West now seek to participate in such a world and to find a place of responsibility in it.

Latin America has a very special place in that world; its historical experiences reflect those which many other countries are passing through in our own times. Problems which it attempted to solve earlier now harass these new countries.

Here in Latin America the necessity has become apparent for an adjustment between its countries and the forces of those interests which in expanding have created demands that should be satisfied. Unfortunately, the requisite adjustment encounters great opposition from forces inimical to the interests of dozens of nations and millions of men. Resistance to these adjustments have produced strains and outbursts of violence which alarm and shake the Americas and seem to surprise our neighbor, the United States. Just such difficulties in adjustment gave rise to the long civil war between France and Algeria, to the earlier conflict in Indochina, and now to the struggle by the United States in Vietnam. Finally, it is an adjustment which arises only through the painful course of the cold war in its spread to the farthest reaches of the world.

The struggle is no longer between socialism and imperialism, but is now between the old imperialism of Europe and areas that are still or were recently its colonies, on the one hand, and, on the other, the new imperialism which seeks to fill the supposed vacuum resulting from the retirement of Europe. The present struggle against colonialism is an old one aroused anew by the contest for world-wide hegemony between the two colossal powers, the United States and the U. S. S. R. The cold war, although extraneous to the old struggle for social adjustment necessary in the Latin American nations in the face of United States or Western expansion, nevertheless complicates it.

Aware of the significance of problems which have arisen and continue to exist in relations between the United States and Latin America—problems that appeared long before the development of the problems that have made it desirable to involve Latin America in the cold war—two economists, one French and one English, asked in somewhat anguished tones, "How have you Latin Americans been able to resist for decades the impact and pressure of the United States which we Europeans, in the relatively short time we have felt it, have found insupportable? . . . Tell us about your experiences, for now they are ours!"

In fact, the entire world—including Western Europe—is undergoing experiences long known to us. In part, these world-wide experiences are similar to those of Latin America suffered in the immediate past under European expansion and to those suffered by the nations formerly European colonies in Asia and Africa. Now Europe itself suffers these same experiences at the hands of its most adept pupil, the United States. In these circumstances, at São Paulo and later conferences, Europeans discovered a common ground with Latin Americans in their complaints, in their exigency for an adjustment of interests, in a confrontation with the Western world now incarnated in the great nation of the northern part of America. Thus the present experiences of Europe and of many other countries are those of Latin America of the present and of the past as well. They, like us, suffer pressures that awaken them and provoke their protests.

Land: The Central Problem of the Americas

III

IT HAS BEEN THE LOT of our generation to live through the beginnings of a world-wide revolution. I refer not only to the Marxian revolution of the proletariat against capitalism but also to a broader and more extensive revolution which preceded it in most non-Western countries—that is, the anticolonial revolution in the marginal countries against the Western powers. According to Toynbee, in all civilizations internal revolutions of the proletariat against their lords and masters have occurred along with the external revolutions of those countries whose roles are that of the proletariat in relation to the great powers. Such was the case of Rome and the barbarians. Rome at last fell victim to the rebellion of those who at that time constituted the marginal countries, the underdeveloped countries, who in one way or another had played a part in the aggrandizement of Rome, giving it not only natural riches but also the strength of the arms of their enslaved sons. Now the same historical development faces Western civilization. Now countries of Asia, Africa, Oceania, and Latin America are those who turn against the West and rebel against a subordination they find unjust. Arnold Toynbee said:

> Even the comparatively feeble native civilization of Mexico is beginning to react. The revolution through which Mexico has been passing since A.D. 1910 may be

interpreted as the first move to shake off the top-dressing of Western civilization which we imposed on Mexico in the sixteenth century; and what is happening today in Mexico may happen tomorrow in the seats of the native civilization of South America: in Peru, Bolivia, Ecuador, and Colombia.[1]

In fact, a similar reaction may occur against Western impositions in countries whose circumstances are like those in Latin America. Latin America has been reacting in a powerful manner in order to overcome not only internal obstacles imposed by its own past but also those put in its way by external forces which impede its Westernization—that is, impede the enjoyment of benefits that the West has revealed to the world, among which are the liberal institutions and fruits of industrialization in the service of those who provide, in addition to the raw products, the labor to transform these.

Latin America reacts to rid itself of the blemishes of that civilization, but not to renounce or oppose its benefits which our countries like others try to make their own. What are those blemishes? We have already indicated their nature, and now restate it in the words of the Asiatic nationalist leader Sukarno, who told his North American listeners in 1956:

One misunderstanding should be eliminated immediately. *We are not anti-West.* We may, in fact we do, sometimes oppose what is called the West. But that is not dictated by a feeling of being anti-West. . . . It is true that there is one manifestation of the West which we—and all of Asia—completely reject and will continue to reject. That manifestation is colonialism.[2]

[1] *Civilization on Trial* (New York, 1949), 221–22.
[2] Address to the National Press Club, Washington, D.C., May 18,

The reaction against colonialism, as we have already indicated, is called nationalism; it is, however, not the aggressive expansionist nationalism that produces imperialism and colonialism but the nationalism that attends solely to its own interests. Certain authoritative voices in Western culture have pointed out, as Toynbee has, that the implied danger of this nationalism is a world that tends more to collaboration than to regional or to some other kind of nationalism. In this connection, Sukarno said: "Perhaps the future belongs to greater organizations than mere nations . . . . In any case, these bodies cannot be built until nations are built first. You can not establish international bodies until nations have established their national identities."[3] None of this will be possible if the injustices imposed by colonialism are not previously ended. Colonialism has not yet disappeared; equal collaboration of all the countries of the world in a common task is not yet a reality. Sukarno continued:

> We have been told that colonialism is dead. . . . My reply to that is a simple one. Come to Asia and see for yourselves. Travel to Africa and see for yourselves. Colonialism, even in its classical form, is *not dead* so long as one nation is unfree, so long as the United Nations Charter is not applied to one territory, so long as brother is divided from brother by a colonial barrier. Colonialism will not be dead until nations—including my nation—are reunited in that freedom which is the birthright of all men.[4]

Another Asiatic nationalist, Nehru of India, took the same point of view when he spoke about his country's

1956. U.S. Department of State *Bulletin*, XXXIV (June 4, 1956), 937.
[3] *Ibid.*, 936.
[4] *Ibid.*, 937.

nationalism and of when it might be possible to abandon it. A nationalistic spirit will cease to exist when it ceases to be a defensive instrument of nations that oppose the aggressive nationalism which has subordinated them and continues to do so. A short time before his country obtained its independence, Nehru wrote that doing so would not imply a complete break with England except with respect to those matters in which England might wish to maintain the old material dominion which must come to an end. He said:

> Such a development in India would be in tune with political and economic internationalism. It would breed no conflicts with other nations and would be a powerful factor for peace in Asia and the world. It would help in the realization of that One World toward which we are inevitably being driven, even though our passions delude us and our minds fail to understand it. The Indian people, freed from the terrible sense of oppression and frustration, will grow in stature again and lose their narrow nationalism and exclusiveness. Proud of their Indian heritage, they will open their minds and hearts to other peoples and other nations, and become citizens of this wide and fascinating world, marching onward with others in that ancient quest in which their forefathers were the pioneers.[5]

Until all this happens, however, nationalism is necessary for countries like ours. "Nationalism," wrote Nehru, "was and is inevitable in the India of my day; it is a natural and healthy growth. For any subject country national freedom must be the first and dominant urge."[6] Nationalism is not yet vanishing in spite of the new international groups and

[5] *The Discovery of India* (New York, 1956), 535.

[6] This quotation and the immediate following are from *ibid.*, 40–42.

36

proletarian movement. Nationalism is still a necessity in such nations as India. "It is still one of the most powerful urges that move a people, and round it cluster sentiments and traditions and a sense of common living and common purpose." These views provide the best point of departure for an internationalism which groups nations according to what they have in common. Nehru added:

Sometimes we are told that our nationalism is a sign of our backwardness and even our demand for independence indicates our narrow mindedness. Those who tell us so seem to imagine that true internationalism would triumph if we agreed to remain as junior partners in the British Empire or Commonwealth of Nations. They do not appear to realize that this particular type of so-called internationalism is only an extension of a narrow British nationalism, which could not have appealed to us even if the logical consequence of Anglo-Indian history had not utterly rooted out its possibility from our minds. Nevertheless, India, for all her intense nationalistic fervor, has gone further than many nations in her acceptance of real internationalism and coordination, and even to some extent the subordination, of the independent nation state in and to a world organization.

Nehru seems to insist that the nationalism of colonial peoples is only a defensive and necessary expression in the face of the nationalism which has been the fruit of imperialism. Only as the latter disappears can the nationalism of colonial countries disappear. There exists among these countries a disposition to collaborate in the great efforts possible on an international basis for transforming the world and making it a happier place for its inhabitants, but never in relation to blocs of interests that benefit only a specific social group or nation.

37

What form of solidarity, then, can this nationalism encompass? It is the kind that we are creating day by day, the kind which countries who manifest certain definite similarities can have among themselves and which can unify them for achieving the greatest success from their efforts. It is the kind which is appearing now among Arab nations in response to Western meddling in the Middle East on the pretext of preventing civil war in Lebanon. Nations not adhering or wishing to adhere to blocs of interests not representative of them are inclined to unify their efforts in the international arena when they see that the menace to a specific country can also become a menace for each of them—that is, they tend to form a definitive union in the face of a common danger. In this connection, Sukarno stated in Mexico:

> We do not adhere to any blocs of powers. We are not members of any military alliance. Our foreign policy is independent and dynamic. But we are not neutral. I repeat, we are not neutral. We shall never be neutral while danger and insecurity exist in the world; while colonization continues to exist in any form whatever; while man goes in fear of that which can put an end to his life and his civilization but which, as an individual, he cannot control. Who can be neutral in this world in this day and time?[7]

Arturo Frondizi, among others in Latin America, has referred to this same type of nationalism, increasingly tied to similar manifestations elsewhere, in these words:

> When the objective is understood, the hour of action has arrived. This is our hour, the hour of countries that in greater or less degree are subjected to the maneuverings

[7] *Novedades* (Mexico City, May 27, 1959).

of imperialism and of internal oligarchies. It is so because in this moment history is really universal history, since men of all geographic regions and of all social sectors demand the right to participate in the creation and enjoyment of material, spiritual, and moral enjoyment as well as scientific and technical benefits. We 170 million human beings who live in Latin America have a veritable privilege in actually struggling for the emancipation of nations and peoples, now that ours is part of the great world-wide struggle which is under way for the purpose of dignifying morally and materially the human state. . . . Anti-imperialism, with a firm emotional and economic base in nationalism, is not a struggle that is limited to one country. The countries of this part of the world especially should include it within the Latin American dimension, but not without recognizing that it relates to a world-wide process of emancipation and of struggles for the achievement of the highest economic standards. This explains the fact that their low levels of development bring together not only the countries of our America but also the distant countries of Asia, Africa, and Oceania, where millions of human beings have problems even more distressing than ours.[8]

Our countries cannot think of despoiling others as a means of promoting their own development. If other countries become menacing, then our attitude can only be a defensive one or, when our problems can be solved among ourselves, a resort to solidarity. In this sense, Latin America and the newly emerging countries in Asia have many problems in common. We all long for some of the fruits of the riches of the soil and of the labor of our sons. This community of interests is becoming apparent and is continuing to be a basis for action. Diplomatic missions sent to far-

[8] *Petróleo y política* (Buenos Aires, 1954), lxi.

39

away countries outwardly foreign to us are evidences of this. For example, the petroleum problems that such Latin American countries as Venezuela, Mexico, Argentina, and Peru have had to face are also problems of the Arab countries that possess this "substance of the devil," as the Mexican poet Ramón López Velarde called it. When a Latin American—specifically a Venezuelan—was present at a meeting in Egypt in 1959, it was the first time in the history of Latin America or of Asia that a representative of Latin America participated in a meeting held by non-Western petroleum-producing countries. The statement of the constitutional president of Venezuela relative to that participation is significant in connection with the point of view expounded here. He said:

Our interest coincides with that of the countries of the Middle East in the common objective of maintaining the price of petroleum in international markets at a high and remunerative level for the producers of this raw product. For this reason, this government extends a diplomatic gesture to the countries of the Middle East without, however, any intention of meddling in matters which are their private concern, even though we share their point of view.[9]

At a meeting in Geneva in 1964 concerning the great economic problems of the world, the creation, by the union of representatives of Asia and Africa along with those of Latin America, of the famous group of seventy-five, by its very numbers, obliged the most obstinate colonial nations to accept, although reluctantly, its point of view on achieving development or simply on remaining undeveloped. Various Latin American countries have also participated in

[9] Rómulo Betancourt, *El Nacional* (Caracas), January 13, 1960.

meetings of Asiatics and Africans such as the one held recently in Cairo. These meetings brought together nations which, without tolerating blocs that might limit them, are participating effectively in diverse international bodies.

Common problems may have common solutions. Problems of Latin America are those of many countries which, like us, strive to conquer the economic, social, and political backwardness in which they find themselves in contrast to the Western world. That inequality provokes the crises in which we now live and produces the menaces shaped by the cold war waged by the great powers in their efforts to maintain the established inequality and furthermore, to take advantage of that inequality to expand their influence. In this connection, Adolfo López Mateos, then president of Mexico, said before the Organization of American States on October 12, 1959: "This crisis consists fundamentally in the disequilibrium which constantly becomes more evident and more extreme between our nearly perfect political institutions and the lacerating social and economic reality of the Latin American nations."[10] The economic and social situations in which these nations find themselves are not compatible with the ideals and the standards for which they should strive. The adopted political institutions are at variance with the material reality on which they depend. On the one hand, there is what our countries want; on the other, what they can do. Obviously, some of these countries have made progress, but their development still stumbles because of a series of difficulties which curb them, making tyranny possible. Concerning these countries, López Mateos said:

Some find themselves in a process of development, while

[10] This quotation and the immediate following from addresses by López Mateos are from *Novedades*, October 12, 1959.

others have scarcely begun; but whatever may be the differences of degree that separate them, all or almost all face similar problems. It is a matter of expanding economics coming up against two obstacles: a great demographic growth in itself a problem, and the lack of resources for financing economic development with the rapidity which the increase of population as much as the necessity of elevating the standard of living demands.

In further development of his ideas of causes that have produced tension among nations, he said, in speaking before the United Nations:

Those causes are misery, injustice, and fear. Misery is frequently the inability of man to take advantage of the resources of nature; injustice is at times the power of oppression of some groups by others; fear usually originates from the menacing of some by others, of the powerful among themselves, or of the weak by the powerful.

We in Latin America, like many in Asia and Africa, are living witnesses of the impediments our countries encounter in the effort to attain the minimum development which could put an end to many of the problems of misery that oppress us in addition to the undeniable increase in population. Our masses increase in spite of misery and consequently increase the minimum demands requisite for mere survival. These demands are the ones least understood by the countries that also have a stake in the future in which all interests are interlaced.

The principal problem of Latin America, as of Asia and Africa, continues to be the problem of landownership. On its solution depends the achievement of the industrialization which will enable Latin America to make itself independent economically as it has been able to make itself

42

independent of the European mother countries in at least a relatively political manner.

Count Hermann Keyserling called our Latin America the Continent of the Third Day of Creation. Earlier the Prussian DePauw and the Frenchman Georges L. L. Buffon had called it the Humid Continent and had considered it immature in relation to the Old World. Hegel did not concede it any role except in the future—which has not yet arrived. The common theme of these opinions was the natural but, at the same time, the historical and cultural backwardness of this America. Latin Americans have discerned their own backwardness while maintaining the ideal of progress. Thus Sarmiento saw civilization as the goal to attain, in opposition to barbarism, the condition that actually prevailed. The Mexican José María Mora, in a similar view, contrasted progress and retrogression—that which is longed for with actuality. The Chilean Bilbao expressed the contrast in terms of modernity versus feudalism. This conflict continues to exist in our own time between the Latin America that is and the one it longs to be. Today, as yesterday, our countries strive to overcome obstacles that impede them and to transform the actuality that makes the continent seem still to be the one of the Third Day of Creation. Our countries want with mounting fervor to incorporate themselves into the stream of progress which is expressed, from the social and economic point of view, in the shift from an agrarian to an industrial society. Latin America and other parts of the world do not want to be simply providers of raw materials and consumers of merchandise that they have not been able to manufacture from those materials. They wish to be owners of their own natural resources and to possess the instruments for transforming these into the goods which will meet their needs.

43

This step, if it is to be taken, will involve a profound change in matters concerning landholding. A society still in a feudal stage of development with respect to land tenure must change that system in order to be able to elevate the standard of living of the masses who constitute the majority in our countries. That change is necessary if the masses are to become both producers of natural wealth and consumers of that wealth transformed by the necessary process of industrialization. Land cannot remain idle as in the past, and even less can it remain in a few hands. Such concentration of ownership is even less desirable if those hands are foreign to the countries where the land is and to whom the fruits of the land belong. On the one hand, it is necessary that the land produce at the maximum rate—no longer merely at the minimum, as it does in accord with the colonial system we have inherited; on the other hand, it is necessary, once maximum production is achieved, to prevent those products from remaining in the possession of foreigners who are indifferent to the exhaustion of the land and to the future misery of the people to whom the products really belong.

This transformation—this step from a rural to an industrial society—encounters obstacles, as might be expected, placed in its way by old interests that continue serving the old colonial regime of exploitation and by other obstacles, relatively new, thrown up by the interests of those countries that augment their prosperity at the cost of the misery of others. These lands and their products must provide the basis for economic and social transformation. In many parts of America they are held not only by old *caciques* and feudal masters but also by Western companies which extract the raw materials subsequently transformed into manufactured goods by their own industries, then sold and resold at great profit to the very people who were their

44

original owners and who are in this manner doubly fleeced. Both the *caciques* and the companies possessing latifundia are opposed to any landholding change that might lead to the end of their established monopolies.

This is the central problem of our America and one which continues to harass other countries that have not overcome the backwardness evidenced by their lack of control over their own resources and their inability to convert and consume these resources. This problem concerns those countries that do not want to be left in a feudal state but want to be industrialized. We insist that it is the prime problem of Africa, the Middle East, Asia, and Oceania, as well as of Latin America. The nationalistic revolutions in these areas must first solve the problem of landholding and achieve agrarian reform before the countries can be incorporated into the march of progress. The requisite reforms involve open war with the double interests, internal and external, that oppose their realization.

At present the problem is more urgent than at any time since the Mexican Revolution of 1910. Other Latin American countries, once they threw out the mercenary dictatorships that had surrendered them to foreign interests, have now faced the necessity of achieving agricultural reform in order to make possible their economic transformation. This reform has already been undertaken in such countries as Venezuela, has caused the revolution in Cuba, has been formulated elsewhere, and will eventually be undertaken in the rest of Latin America in one form or another, depending on local circumstances. In some countries—for example, Cuba—reform has met with intense resistance. Those who oppose it accept the desired political changes, which, after all, will prove ineffective unless these are accompanied by social transformation, but they resist by every possible

45

means the agrarian reform on which the efficacy of political transformation must depend.

I have called attention to the fact that agrarian reform provokes revolts and ferocious counterrevolutions, clearly demonstrated in Guatemala in 1954. From the beginning of its revolution in 1910, Mexico has encountered this same sort of resistance, thus revealing to the people that changes in the system of landholding are at the very core of what must be their genuine revolution. We should take note of Mexico's experiences in her revolution in matters concerning land which, without regard to either skill or error in handling them, have enabled her to achieve social and economic transformation and to enter that stage of industrialization which is the goal of the so-called undeveloped countries.

Arnold Toynbee believes that this agrarian reform must occur in all non-Western countries and that it is the key to their revolutions. The solution of the land problem will provide the desired point of departure for the industrialization of non-Western countries and for their incorporation into Western civilization as something other than mere providers of raw materials who, with their misery, sustain the prosperity of great nations.

Toynbee considered the Mexican Revolution of 1910 the best example of the nationalistic revolutions now spreading throughout the world. This kind of social and economic movement must become general in non-Western countries that are still in a feudal state not only in Latin America but elsewhere. Toynbee wrote in 1952:

Since 1910 the Mexican nation has been playing a distinctive role in the common life of our Western civilization. . . . The agrarian revolution in Mexico in 1910 interests me particularly, because I think that, in this, the

46

Mexican people have been pioneers. What has been accomplished in Mexico already in this field might, perhaps, happen also in other Latin American countries, and perhaps in Asia and Africa as well. The Mexican agrarian revolution, besides being immensely interesting in itself, seems to me to be an historic event. I see in it the beginning of a world-wide movement.[11]

What Toynbee said at that time is being realized with astonishing exactitude in various parts of the world. The revolution in Latin America is in the initial stage of those developments which will enable it to cease being the continent of the Third Day of Creation, a land of a degree of immaturity that exposes it to all kinds of exploitation. Many of the new and increasingly active groups now coming forward, those which may be called nationalistic middle classes, are beginning to view the matter in this light. These groups are now sufficiently knowledgeable to realize the necessity for agrarian revolution as the basis for the most likely achievement of that progress and prosperity. Such social groups, like their Western models, have not been able to prosper by supporting themselves through the misery of foreign peoples; but neither can they profit from the misery of their own people, because doing so would simply prepare the way for their own misery. That is, these groups know that the industrialization they hope for would be just another utopian dream if they lack markets in which to offer their products. Such markets would be difficult to find outside their own nations because of the opposition they would meet from already established and better organized interests. They can never find such markets in their own countries if the majority of the people have scarcely enough to keep themselves alive. In short, industrialization depends basic-

[11] Arnold Toynbee to the author, December 11, 1952.

47

ally on the elevation of the standard of living of the people, who must be the principal body of consumers. We see social groups, now aware of this fact, coming to the fore in our America, as well as in nations elsewhere. The nationalistic bourgeoisie understand now that their progress through industrialization cannot rise from the weak foundation of a miserable agrarian population. In this connection, López Mateos said on undertaking his candidacy for the Mexican presidency: "The achievement of maximum progress by our country requires sacrifices that should not fall on only one group of Mexicans for the benefit of others. The sacrifice and the benefit must be general because the strengthening and the accelerated constant development of our country are."[12]

It is obvious that our people must make sacrifices in order to pay for their industrialization and progress. The progress of Western countries was paid for by sacrifices of other peoples, but there are none who can pay for ours. It is something for which we ourselves must pay; what is more, all must pay, not just a specific group, not just a weak majority, but all social groups without exception. It is necessary to work and to make sacrifices, but on an equal basis, with an equal distribution of sacrifices and benefits in such a manner that all the members of our nations without exception will experience the growth of their nations as an expression of their own growth, and will see their sacrifices as necessary for the achievement of that growth which, though national, must have concrete expression in themselves.

What is said about the national arena may be said also about the international. Because the economies of all countries are bound together, the exploitation of the misery

[12] *Novedades,* November 17, 1957.

of one group of countries for the achievement of prosperity among the more privileged must not continue. The misery of the majority can end by becoming the misery of the minority; the misery of the weak will become that of the powerful. Although our most dynamic and progressive groups are beginning to understand this, it is not yet understood by the representatives of interests of other countries that try to increase or maintain their prosperity through the classic exploitation of the masses in other countries. The latter fail to consider what is happening or has happened in times of crises when exploitation and consequent misery react on prosperity based on a weak foundation. Misery and a low standard of living eliminate the possible consumers of their manufactured goods and, in the process, the possibility of employment and prosperity for their own people who would eventually increase the ranks of the miserable. Eventually, only misery can rise out of misery.

Those who prefer rapid enrichment without regard to the consequences find this hard to understand. They are the ones who would kill the goose that laid the golden eggs, believing that in its dead body they will find a mine of riches beyond imagination. They are the avaricious ones who are so impatient that they are not satisfied with the natural wealth which is the result of attention to, and care of, the elements which make it possible. The result of their impatience is the destruction of the source of prosperity and wealth. Those who out of greed deal misery and death to the ones who were the source of that wealth bring down misery and death on themselves as well. This is the sort of situation that produces obstacles which countries such as ours encounter in trying to achieve that minimum of security which would permit them to be active participants in the progress and prosperity of which the great nations speak.

49

Our countries must achieve a basic minimum of reform—for example, agrarian reform. At this very moment, their achievement faces curbs and obstacles raised against any reform which mean the least alteration of the internal and external interests that have based their prosperity on the maintenance of those obstacles. Thus agrarian reform, which is the basis of the prosperity and the strengthening of the undeveloped countries, meets with the most powerful impediments. In order to curb and prevent this strengthening, a thousand pretexts have been sought, a thousand and one justifications. The principal support of these pretexts and justifications has been found in the cold war—that is, in the struggle against communism. The accusation of being Communist is leveled not against active members of the Communist party—but against any individual that tries to achieve the least degree of social and economic reform. Activists in the cold war will consider agrarian reform—so urgently needed in Latin America, as in all undeveloped countries or those in the process of development—within the Communist line, and will, in the name of democracy, liberty, and security of the Americas or of any other continent, combat it and persecute its supporters.

Conditions imposed by the Alliance for Progress for receiving aid is one of many demonstrations that agrarian reform is a necessity. President John F. Kennedy, author of the Alliance, was clearly conscious of this necessity and for that reason made it a condition the lack of which would render useless the aid of the United States in the effort to raise the standard of living in Latin America. Nevertheless, other forces saw this reform not as one to be encouraged but, rather, as one to be resisted, and ascribed to it the stigma of communism.

Shortly before the Kennedy administration showed the

necessity for agrarian reform, the Cuban Revolution found it necessary to align itself with the Communist bloc of nations in order to subsist and to avoid following the road traveled by other nations like Guatemala and thus becoming a pawn in causes beyond its national interest—a pawn in the cold war. Thereafter we saw the fall of Latin American governments which tried under the stimulus of the Alliance for Progress to achieve timid reforms; these governments were immediately attacked as menaces to the free world and to the security of the Americas.

Latin America and the Cold War

IV

Soon after the end of World War II, the United States and the U. S. S. R., the two great victorious powers, engaged in a covert struggle for hegemony which has been labeled the "cold war." Its object has been to extend economic and ideological dominion, particularly over the new nations that have arisen with the termination of the military conflict or from the displacement of the old imperialist powers. The struggle spread, with the same aims, to include such old conflicts as that between Latin American nationalism and United States expansionism.

The cold war became critical in connection with crises in Korea, Berlin, the Middle East, and Asia. North American lack of understanding of Latin America's problems and of its determination to define its interests with respect to the cold war led to the Cuban policy whereby a nationalist revolution was converted into a Communist one. As a consequence Cuba became linked through a natural instinct for survival with one of the contenders in the cold war. That same cold war threatened earlier, in Korea and Berlin, to become heated to the point of explosion into a world-wide catastrophe. Now that threat exists in Vietnam and Cuba. Even though no one wishes to bring about such an outcome, each of the great powers uses the dread possibility as an instrument to deter its opponent and to force Latin American countries to enter the orbit of one or the other of the opponents.

The cold war has been accompanied by an extraordinary display of sophisticated new weapons capable of destroying the world in a few hours. We note the deterrent nature of these weapons, but recognize that their potential danger lies in the possibility that the antagonistic powers could lose control of them through some accident that would result in catastrophe. First came the race for control of atomic energy and the making of bombs, with each new one more powerful than the one before. The periodic testing of these bombs has led to world-wide protests, not only because of their direct implications but also because of the resultant poisoning of the atmosphere which endangers the health of humanity and causes hardly imaginable future ills.

Next came the race to produce guided missiles, which reached its peak in the sending of artificial satellites into outer space. As a result of that achievement, flights of astronauts and space ships followed. These could be useful to mankind as instruments for greater achievements in space. For the great competing powers, however, they are no more than means for frightening humanity and extending their unquestioned dominion over the earth. Atomic energy, directed missiles, and space ships are not yet, unfortunately for our world, anything more than the bludgeons of primitive man. Such scientific advances in conjunction with the cold war reveal to the combatants just what a hot war could mean.

The most alert elements of public opinion in the United States have exerted pressure to end the struggle, which, if intensified, could bring about the destruction of the world. The propaganda that shapes opinion behind the Iron Curtain has recognized the potential danger of the situation,

53

pointing out the necessity for maintaining peace and repudiating any undertaking that would put in it danger. In spite of the armament race, neither the United States nor the U. S. S. R. indicates a disposition to assume responsibility for starting a destructive and total war. In 1962, the Caribbean crisis, provoked by the installation of Soviet directed missiles in Cuba, made evident this desire for peace by the rival powers in spite of the power competition in which they are engaged.

President Kennedy and Prime Minister Khrushchev sought an accord which would rule out the possibilities of a war that neither wanted. In this agreement the particular interests of Cuba were, on the whole, marginal. It continued to be a pawn in the cold war, useful only in accordance with the interests of the players. There was no lack, however, of opposition in both camps to the agreement and the compromises on which the two great powers had been able to come together. On one side, the assassination of President Kennedy and the candidacy of Barry Goldwater, with his return to the language of deterrence, and, on the other, the Chinese reaction against Russian policy, culminating in the fall of Khrushchev—these were evidences of attitudes that ran counter to an awareness of the dangers of the cold war. But the defeat of Goldwater by Lyndon B. Johnson, heir of the Kennedy policy, and the attitude taken by the new Soviet leaders toward following the pacifist policy of their predecessor in spite of Chinese pressure were highly indicative of the desire of both powers to put an end to, or at least to diminish the fervor of, the cold war. Does this indicate a peaceful partition of the world-wide hegemony of those powers?

What is going to happen in Latin America? Will there be the pretexts offered by the cold war for maintaining the status quo which suits the interests of the United States in this part of the world? Everybody knows—and I emphasize —that the problems discussed in Latin America are the old ones that antedate those growing out of the cold war and, on the whole, antedate the organization of communism as a militant doctrine. The problems of Latin America in its relations with the United States are as old as its history— they appeared almost as soon as the countries of this continent had declared independence.

The liberators themselves faced these same problems. Bolívar, who strove for the understanding and interest of the United States for his epic undertaking of the liberation of Spanish America, soon discovered what he could expect. "How many frustrated hopes!" he wrote in his famous letter from Jamaica. "Not only the Europeans but even our own brothers to the North have remained indifferent spectators of this conflict, which by its very nature is a most just one."[1] That country, he said in effect to his friend Guillermo White, will do nothing that does not conform to its interests: "North America, in accordance with its businesslike conduct of affairs, will take advantage of the occasion to acquire Florida, our friendship, and extensive commercial dominion."[2] That country still showed interest in this America, but only in relation to its interests, an attitude of which the Monroe Doctrine has been clear evidence. That America of Washington and Jefferson, in spite of being champions of liberty, would still do nothing to promote it, outside its own society, that did not conform to its

[1] Simón Bolívar, "Contestación de un americano meridional a un caballero de esta isla," Kingston, Jamaica, September 6, 1815. *Obras Completas*. Compilación y notas de Vicente Lecuna, con la colaboración de la Señorita Barret de Nazaris. 2 vols. Ministro de Educación Nacional de los Estados Unidos de Venezuela (Havana, 1947), I, 162.

[2] May 1, 1820, *ibid.*, II, 429.

interests. "The United States," Bolívar wrote with bitterness to Patrick Campbell, "seems destined by Providence to plague America with misery in the name of liberty."[3]

The same problem recognized by Bolívar in 1829 continues to exist. Latin America still suffers dictatorships, plunderings, attacks, and all kinds of crimes, just as it did before, in the name of a theoretical freedom foreign to it. The cold war has made available new pretexts which have enabled the interests of which Bolívar spoke to grow and be protected. Today, just as yesterday, intervention in Latin America continues in the name of freedom. Yesterday, in the name of freedom, the object ostensibly was to prevent European despotism from intervening in the name of the Holy Alliance. Now, also in the name of freedom, the pretext is to prevent the intervention of Communist despotism led by Russia, but, in either case, to prevent anything that could mean a limitation of the interests of that country even when the effort at limitation emanates from the very country that suffers the imposition of those interests. In one way or another the efforts of Latin America to emancipate itself economically have always been linked with an alleged foreign intervention considered hostile to the American continents if those efforts were contrary to the interests of the United States.

Thus, the cold war, and the struggle against European despotism in the past and against communism in the present have been good slogans for justifying North American intervention in Latin America. It is evident that there have been epochs, as in the time of Theodore Roosevelt, when the United States intervened openly in the name of menaced North American interests. Nevertheless, to the degree that North American expansion through the world

[3] August 5, 1829, *ibid.*, II, 737.

has increased, it has been more and more under pressure to seek moral justifications to prevent loss of prestige among countries that may enter its orbit of influence. Starting with the two great world wars, which coincided with its pinnacle and predominance, the United States had to uphold high principles in the struggle against German despotism, Nazi brutality, and Japanese imperialism. These same principles are now utilized against Communist expansion led by Russia, and necessarily circumscribe open action and oblige the United States to seek justifications that are in accord with the principles it has proclaimed.

The cold war between the United States and the U. S. S. R. has been a marvelous pretext for justifying North American intervention in Latin America in defense of, or for expanding, the interests of its investors. Any action incompatible with these interests is interpreted as an expression of Communist intervention in America and, on that account, a menace to the security of the continent. Efforts that Latin American countries make to improve their economic condition necessarily come up against interests already established or being established by United States investors, provoking the reaction which interferes with the success of those efforts. These countries not only have to struggle against those national interests opposed to any change which would affect their predominance but, what is more, have to face the pressure imposed on them by the representatives of foreign investors whose interests could be affected. Thus a problem as old as that of the land in Latin America is converted into one linked with the cold war which the great powers sustain. Those who resist any agrarian reform will be hailed as supporters of freedom and democracy, while those who dare to proclaim that the land should belong to those who work it will be considered

57

opponents of those principles. Thus we see arrayed on the side of freedom and democracy such advocates as Rafael Trujillo of Santo Domingo, Anastasio Somoza of Nicaragua, Tiburcio Carías of Honduras, Fulgencio Batista of Cuba, Marcos Pérez Jiménez of Venezuela, Gustavo Rojas Pinilla of Colombia, and other bloody tyrants of Latin American countries. On the other side, hailed as dangerous enemies of the security of the continent and therefore as enemies of freedom and democracy, are Lázaro Cárdenas of Mexico, Juan José Arévalo of Guatemala, and other Latin American leaders who have dared to do what the United States and other great powers do—that is, to stand up for the interests of their own countries.

Continental security, democracy, and freedom have simply been turned into pretexts for the justification of intervention which would otherwise appear as pure aggression by strong countries against the weak. Economic and political suppression of Latin American countries have been sought under the cover of these banners. In the face of the supposed Communist menace and in the supposed service of freedom and democracy, many Latin American countries have been obliged to accept military pacts that subordinate them economically as well as militarily and politically. This was revealed by the criticism in Uruguay of a military pact made by that country. Such pacts have required our countries to accept conditions incompatible with their very existence.[4] Thus the cold war is transformed into good business. Far from being a menace, it becomes a useful instrument for promoting special interests and for preventing attacks on any of them. What will happen when this threat fades away and the cold war congeals, if the two great powers reach an accord? Arévalo anticipated that possibility when he said

[4] *Novedades,* July 27, 1960.

that Mars might then represent the menace.[5] The need for world security in the face of the possibility of a Martian invasion could become the new banner.

The Mexican Revolution was one of the first to suffer at the hands of the interests it endangered at a time when the latter did not have the pretext of the cold war. Obviously, these interests ascribed supposedly humanitarian pretexts, such as that of putting an end to the slaughter of Mexicans by Mexicans, in order to condemn the revolution and to make intervention possible. Nevertheless, the agrarian reform of President Cárdenas and the petroleum expropriation provoked reactions reminiscent of the ones now occurring. In that period Russia was already looming as a power that one day might put the great Western powers in the shade. Communism had become a world-wide threat. The Mexican Revolution was openly termed a Communist revolution then, although today a North American ambassador considers it a model to follow in contrast to other revolutions which now turn out to be Communist. Guatemala in 1954 and Cuba more recently exhibit the advantage, already classic, of the cold war for curbing the social and economic transformation of Latin America.

General Cárdenas proclaimed to the world his concurrence with this interpretation of the situation when he supported the Cuban Revolution then under way, in his address of July 26, 1960, at the great popular demonstration in support of Fidel Castro and his proposed agrarian reform. The Cuban Revolution, he said to his million listeners in Havana, was inspired by the most noble principles, especially with respect to agrarian reform. That is the source of the violence against this revolution, of the attacks and

[5] *Ibid.*

calumnies, none of which would have resulted from merely a change of leadership. Cárdenas said:

> Their tactics are not new; opponents of social reforms in our country employed them many years ago. Those same interests inspired the black legend of the Mexican Revolution. They launched all sorts of charges against our people, calling them destroyers of national wealth, disturbers of order, and enemies of civilization. They have accused them falsely ever since of being at the service of foreign governments. . . . The agrarian reform of Mexico has been the object of the most virulent insults from the enemies of the struggle against the feudal regime.[6]

The same tactics are still in use, just as they were used against Guatemala in 1954. Problems peculiar to the nations undertaking the transformation of their social and economic status were tied to the cold war, to which they were outsiders. At the core of the cold war were international conflicts which were used as pretexts, as justification, for putting an end to any endeavor at emancipation or economic recovery. The great powers extended their frontiers to all points of the earth in which the interests of their investors were menaced. Problems raised in this connection which might have been resolved with a minimum of justice and goodwill have been blown up to world-wide significance with no solution possible except complete submission and the suppression of every demand in the name of continental security, peace, liberty, and other principles that had inspired the suppressed demands. In this connection, General Cárdenas, referring to the economics and social recovery of all colonial peoples as well as to the Mexican and Cuban revolutions, said:

[6] Juan José Arévalo, *La Fábula del Tiburón y las Sardinas* (Mexico City, 1956), 121.

Colonial countries that have achieved political autonomy but are still economically weak endure the pressure of great problems which they really want to solve. Each time, however, that they endeavor to take steps along the road of political or economic liberation, they are accused of participating in the cold war. Thus the effort is made to use the actual international tension that the world suffers as a shield to hide the true meaning of the popular struggle for freedom and for the betterment of the conditions of life. . . . We see now that each time the essential rights of citizens or the betterment of conditions of life are claimed, those who make the demands are accused, in the course of the cold war, of serving the faction opposing the United States.[7]

The cold war has been converted into a mechanism at the service of the powers who make use of it not only against their opponents—or against the great opponent—but also against countries that try to make some change involving their interests, no matter how diminished these latter may be. The cold war has been converted into a modus vivendi of numerous interests, the very ones that now see with dismay that it might come to an end. These same interests opposed Khrushchev's visit to the United States. These are the same ones that criticized President Eisenhower for having permitted that visit and for trying to reach an understanding with the Russian premier. These interests opposed the international policy of President Kennedy and that of his successor. They encouraged the appearance of such an extremist candidate as Goldwater. Finally, they have, by diverse means, opposed any understanding between the two great opponents.

Since some, with frankness and appropriate cynicism, have held that the end of the cold war could cause a grave

[7] *Novedades* (Mexico, D. F.), July 27, 1960.

economic crisis in the United States, with a decline in many businesses and a resulting increase in unemployment, it would seem that the hatred, distrust, and fear of the U. S. S. R. and China that Western propaganda has inspired have been pure fabrications. That hatred, distrust, and fear have had no other objective than to maintain the economic stability, which has been resting on the false foundation of the cold war. Members of the power elite, of whom C. Wright Mills speaks, were playing "brinkmanship," fearing not so much a war that would put an end to humanity but the termination of the cold war, which allows them to justify their active intervention in any act that harms their interests. They tremble in fear of the end of the cold war because it might alter the economic structure reared upon it. No one wishes a "hot war"; everyone wants peace—but a peace which would maintain without change the numerous interests created in the name of the cold war.

On that account, Latin American countries and others that find themselves in a similar situation—as well as Western countries, including the United States—see, in spite of the optimism that recent international events have engendered, as so much utopian dreaming the hope of actually ending the cold war. It has, in one way or another, served the opposing powers without their having to reach the point that would mean heating it up. Through the cold war, the United States has strengthened and increased its interests even to the point—apparent in the Middle East and Asia—of displacing her old Western allies. The U. S. S. R., in the circumstances of that same war, has made itself secure in the area it had reached at the end of World War II and, at the same time, has succeeded in increasing its prestige and consequently the acceptance of its doctrines among colonial and semicolonial nations that have endured pressures from the West.

The United States and the U. S. S. R.—enemies sustaining antagonistic doctrines and attitudes—have seemed, nevertheless, to have been in accord in maintaining the cold war because of the favorable consequences to the interests and goals of each. For one, the central preoccupation is economic; for the other, political. Both—although it seems paradoxical—have achieved success in their intermediate or immediate objectives. In the Middle East, for example, the United States, in the name of security of the world and of Western values, has succeeded in filling the vacuum left by England and France as it has in Asia and Oceania, where it has replaced Holland. As a consequence, however, of this action, which has strengthened the United States economy, the political influence of the U. S. S. R. has been strengthened in these same regions in which North America has expanded. The United States has increased its economic power in combating communism at the same time that the U. S. S. R. has expanded its political influence —hence the damage which capitalism may suffer as a consequence of its struggle against communism.

In Latin America also, we have endured this domination, this game of contending for advantage in which the cost falls on the countries that serve as prize or booty rather than on the adversaries. The cold war here, as in the rest of the world subject to the struggle for dominion, has served to curb any nationalist demands on the pretense that these demands are only forms of pressure by international communism which it is necessary to resist. The most obvious and urgent demands have been denied, and those who presented the demands have been accused of being Com-

63

munists and followers of interests foreign to the continent. Consequently, communism has gained prestige, and the U. S. S. R. has achieved not only influence among thousands of discontented Latin Americans but also moral triumphs of propaganda among other non-Western countries—that is, political triumphs that have threatened to heat up the cold war.

In Guatemala, in Cuba, and in other countries that struggle for their own interests, the pressures have been double: both capitalist interests and Communist agents have applied pressure to achieve a situation that would be, paradoxically, advantageous to both. Increase of the Communist pressure to a degree that could be used to justify the intervention desired by the capitalist interests permitted that double triumph. United Fruit and many other interests foreign to Guatemala were made secure and all efforts at national recovery crushed. Communism, however, and with it the U. S. S. R., gained prestige. The United States suffered a great moral—that is, political—defeat of which the troubled journey of Vice-President Nixon gave ample evidence. Both contenders achieved their goals, and the only loser—the one sacrificed—was Guatemala. Everybody denounced the "villain" that, though trampling its own principles underfoot, had given the *coup de grâce* to the small Central American republic; but the interests that incited that villainy remain in the sacrificed nation stronger than ever.

Shortly thereafter the game was repeated, this time in Hungary. There the provocateurs were the standard bearers of democracy who provoked the popular uprising against the U. S. S. R. in order to use it later as a moral propaganda tool against communism and its crimes. In the meantime the U. S. S. R. completely suppressed the nationalistic uprising and made itself secure politically. The cold war, in these instances as well as in others, served only to allow the two contenders to reaffirm their positions in the area of greatest interest to each. It was a cold war always held back from the point where it could be a serious threat to one or the other of the great contenders, that could be halted at the moment it might injure either and not merely the other countries that might suffer its consequences. In recent months that cold war has reached such a dangerous degree of heat that the very existence of the contenders has been in the balance. What is desired is the elimination of the cold war or at least some adjustments which would perhaps allow retention of its advantages without its dangers.

Such is the nature of the international scene and a possible consequence of the accord which might be achieved by the two great powers for whom the cold war has served as a means of maintaining and increasing their economic and political positions. The interests that have achieved power through the cold war will not accept its termination if that means that they might be curbed or, at least, made insecure. Measures will be adopted to satisfy the demands for peace and the security of Western countries, but care will be taken that the economic status based on the cold war does not change.

In any event, termination of the cold war will not indicate the end or the limitation of the interests that have created that status.

The U. S. S. R. would of course gladly accept a solution which would permit an end to a cold war that requires so many economic sacrifices by its people; as we have been informed, the Russian economy is at the service of political goals. After all, the U. S. S. R. knows by experience that, to the degree that capitalism exerts its pressure on other countries, the political influence of communism, and therefore that of the U. S. S. R. will grow. The end of the cold war would end only the dangers of a mortal war between the great powers; it would not end the economic and political pressures suffered by the underprivileged nations of the world.

A Latin American statesman, in commenting on the possibility of the conclusion of the cold war, declared, "With the cold war or without it, the big fish will continue eating the little fish." Here may be found the crux of the solution of that unavoidable fact. How long are the Latin American countries going to continue being merely little fish? According to the ancient thesis of the Sophist Callicles, it is a law of nature that to be alive is the highest good. But to the claim that law is on the side of the strongest, Socrates responded that the force which surges from the union of those who are weak but isolated can be strong if bound together, like the strength of straws bound together in a broom. Socrates asked whether it did not conform to nature that many men together are more powerful than the isolated man. The proof is that the many impose laws on the individual.

And what is true of individuals is true of nations. Why have our countries not been able to unite, in some manner that does not injure their sovereignty and personality, in order to aid in achieving that peace sought for in the end of the cold war? Why do we not unify our forces with those of many other countries of the world who have also been cast in the role of little fish to feed the big ones? That union should not be for the purpose of imposing certain interests upon others but only for exacting respect for ourselves. There is still alive the old Bolivarian ideal of seeking the unity of our countries in order that through this unity they

66

may be able to enter into collaboration with other peoples of the world—even the great powers, in a role other than that of being little fish to feed the voracity of the big ones.

The exigencies of the new China are being added now to those of the great powers of the East and the West. On the unification of its people, China has ceased being the little fish of the recent past and now demands that the powers take her into account if there is really to be peace undisturbed by any war, hot or cold. Why have our countries not been able to be an equal part in this world of peace that is coming into sight? Why not Latin America? Why not the rest of Asia? Why not Oceania? That is, why not the whole world? Latin America and the rest of the world that is subject to the hazardous games of the disputes between the great powers do not have to remain in the situation assigned them by the great powers if they create through union a new power structure. Something of the kind is beginning to emerge in various parts of the world. There are already various instances of, at least, moral solidarity that are being experienced among nations. Only by shifting from a passive attitude to an active search for solidarity will our countries be able to emerge from under the pressures that otherwise they will continue to suffer, with or without the cold war. Only then will they be able to play an active part in the preparation of a permanent peace which, in order to be permanent, must count on the collaboration of all the peoples of the world without discrimination.

What Does Latin America Want?

V

WHEN NASSER'S POSITION was becoming most difficult, the nationalistic Arab leader appealed to North American public opinion by pointing out that the Arabs wished nothing for themselves that Americans had not previously demanded. The Arabs, he said, had no desire to promote communism or any doctrine contrary to the ideals of the West but to do only what Americans undertook in 1776 in endeavoring to emerge from the colonial state—neither more nor less. (All colonial peoples can make that reply to that public when it expresses surprise at agitation of the sort its ancestors lived through nearly two centuries ago.)

Actually, July 4, 1776, launched a movement which resulted also in independence for the Latin American countries and for almost all other countries that had been colonies of Western nations. The English colonies refused to continue serving as a means for promoting the prosperity and progress of the mother country. They did not wish to continue accepting the mercantilist policy of the English crown, for it violated the civil and political rights which the colonies had inherited from England. The English policy subordinated the interests of the colonies in order to increase those of the mother country and thereby hindered their development. Onerous taxes and numerous commercial restrictions which hampered the colonies finally became insupportable.

The Declaration of Independence of the United States was based on the philosophy expressed in the following statement:

> We hold these truths to be self-evident, that all men are created equal; that they are endowed by their Creator with certain inalienable rights; that among these are life, liberty, and the pursuit of happiness. That, to secure these rights, governments are instituted among men, deriving their just powers from the consent of the governed; that, whenever any form of government becomes destructive of these ends, it is the right of the people to alter or abolish it, and to institute a new government, laying its foundation on such principles, and organizing its powers in such form, as to them shall seem most likely to effect their safety and happiness.

The first democratic nation of the world was erected in America on the basis of these principles. Other nations, even in Europe itself, followed its example and were inspired by its principles. France received on the rebound the achievement of the ideals of its philosophers; inspired by those principles, it emancipated itself from the clerical and feudal orders which curbed its development, and inaugurated a new form of government with the triumph of the revolution.

Inspired by one or the other of these revolutions, the Latin American countries attempted to follow in the footsteps of these nations. They achieved independence from their European origins, but they failed to put into effect the principles of the American Revolution which would have transformed them into a great nation or group of nations. Such an achievement has been impeded, in the first place, by these countries' cultural heritage, the principles of which were not those of the new philosophy. Unlike the United States, they did not inherit a body of civil rights and policies which could be used in their own defense as justification of their rebellion, as inspiration for their emancipation.

The principles set forth in the Declaration of Independence of the United States were repeated in the declarations framed by the countries of Latin America signalizing their own independence. Those principles were, however, no more than sentimental and unworkable statements in the face of the actual reality of Latin America, no more than a collection of expressions of hope about what they wanted their countries to be, in a simple spirit of imitation that did not coincide with the social, political, cultural, or economic reality to which they wished to apply these principles. Alexis de Tocqueville interpreted the situation from this point of view when he referred to the inutility of adapting such principles for the new Latin American nations in an effort to transform them into democracies similar to the North American nation. "The Constitution of the United States," he said, "is like one of those exquisite productions of human industry which insure wealth and renown to their inventors, but which are profitless in any other hands."[1]

To the natural difficulty arising from the differences in the spirit of the heritage of Latin America, another must be added—that occasioned by the expansion of the West over the world, soon epitomized by the United States itself when it was transformed into a powerful nation determined to grow, like other Western nations, at the expense of others.

[1] *Democracy in America.* Translated by Henry Reeve (2 vols., New York, 1899), I, 162.

By the second half of the nineteenth century, the United States, the great model democracy, had become another agent of Western expansion over the rest of the world. First England, France, and Holland, then the United States, imposed their wills on Latin America, Asia, and Africa, just as England had done to an extreme degree on what had been her colony in the New World.

Thus these Western nations, in their relations with Latin America, Asia, and Africa, not only violated the political and civil rights which they claimed for themselves but they did more—they did not even acknowledge that those rights belonged to others. The United States, on justifying her rebellion against England, listed a series of grievances similar to those which non-Western countries suffered in the course of Western expansion. Not only was the development of non-Western nations curbed but forces were stimulated which could wipe out any development. The means was the maintenance of a feudal or semifeudal state in which these countries existed upon becoming subjected to the forces of expansion. England, France, and Holland supported puppet kings, *caciques*, and tyrants in Asia, Africa, and Oceania at the same time that the United States was following a similar policy in Latin America.

Latin America, after enduring tyrants and *caciques* who undertook to occupy the places of viceroys and governors who left when independence was achieved, had then to endure *caciques*, tyrants, and dictators created and supported by the nation which had served as a model. The natural riches of Latin America, like those of other colonial areas, far from contributing to the well-being of their own people, became their greatest misfortune. Conservative dictators and personal rulers gave way to mercenary dictators at the service of the powerful interests of Western expansion. Putting into effect the principles Latin Americans had sentimentally copied and incorporated at the heads of their declarations of independence seemed, to Latin America and to other regions in similar circumstances, farther away than ever.

Nevertheless, we are now witnessing an extraordinary transformation in countries that only yesterday were colonies or semicolonies of the West. World War II, in which the proclaimed principles of the North American Declaration of Independence and of the free and democratic nations were triumphant over one of the most brutal and dehumanized dictatorships, was a strong stimulus for the countries which had been denied the right to proclaim and realize those principles. Countries whose sons died on battlefields in many parts of the world for these standards made them their own after that triumph. Many, having already proclaimed their adherence to those principles, now demand recognition of their right to their achievement. Today, India, China, Burma, Indonesia, Lebanon, Syria, Egypt, Tunis, and Algeria—as well as the countries of black Africa and the parts of Africa still under the dominion of England, France, and Belgium—adhere to the same standards which nearly two centuries ago were proclaimed by another colony which has now become one of the great democratic powers of the world.

Nehru made this point when he explained the nationalistic movement which brought about India's independence. India accepted principles for which her people had died on the battlefield and had made their own through their sacrifices. In August, 1942, India was already moving in the direction of casting off the Western yoke. Western democracies had appealed for aid from Asia and Africa in defense of these same principles. In spite of the war and of the requested sacrifice, the Western powers were not willing to concede to colonial countries the principles and rights for which the sons of these countries were dying. Nehru wrote:

> But, as the war developed, it became ever clearer that the Western democracies were fighting not for a change but for a perpetuation of the old order. . . . Political democracy in western Europe and North America, opening the door to national and individual progress, had also released new forces and new ideas, aiming inevitably at economic equality. Conflict was inherent in the situation; there would either be an enlargement of that political democracy or attempts to curb and end it.[2]

The growth of democracy necessarily affected the interests of the groups which had benefited economically by it. Consequently, Nehru said, these groups cried to the high heavens when other men and other peoples increased their demands. In countries where democracy had not yet been put into effect, Western powers sought allies in curbing democracy among the groups always opposed to it. According to Nehru, "So it was a natural consequence for these Western democracies to feel some kind of an ideological bond with fascism, even when they disliked many of its more brutal and vulgar manifestations." Put on the defensive by fascist aggression, the Western nations did not lose their fear of a resurgence of the peoples in their colonies that might limit their interests, and they struggled on as if it were a war in defense of those interests instead of one in favor of the principles crushed by fascism.

Other peoples, however—many others whose interests were not directly threatened by the war—struggled and died

[2] This quotation and the immediate following are from *The Discovery of India* (New York, 1956), 490–91.

73

to make a reality of the principles of democracy menaced by those who had initiated the war. Nehru said:

> And there were those hundreds of millions of the dispossessed and exploited and racially discriminated-against in Europe and America, and even more so in Asia and Africa who could not isolate the war from their memories of the past and from their present misery, and passionately hoped, even when hope was unreasonable, that the war would somehow lift the burdens that crushed them.

As a consequence, rebellion broke out when those hopes were wiped out by the Western democracies, who viewed the war only as a defense of their interests and assumed that their triumph in the war would mean restoration of their interests.

Latin America suffered similar deceptions. The triumph of the democracies over the totalitarian Axis, far from promoting democracy in our countries, represented a retrogression. The few democracies that managed to appear at the end of the war were quickly suppressed by the Creole militarism stimulated by the interests of the democracies that were triumphant in the world. In Argentina, Peru, Colombia, Venezuela, Cuba, and Guatemala, dictators were added to the ones already existing, and the countries which succeeded in upholding the principles of democracy found themselves in a difficult and precarious situation. The democracy that had triumphed in the war was hidden from those countries. In spite of everything, however, the same spirit that had animated the liberators of the United States, the same spirit that had moved our liberators, continued to live among our peoples.

Therefore, that spirit of democratization of which Africa and Asia have become aware had to be reborn in Latin

America, which could not be insensible to the movement of national democratization which its forefathers had wanted. Nationalism in Latin America, similar to that in North Africa, black Africa, Indonesia, India, and many other places, has been evident since the 1910 Mexican Revolution. In one way or another, this movement has found expression in the rest of Latin America in spite of impediments and obstacles that certain interests, which realize they are affected, put in its way. This same movement has begun in recent years to rid itself of the embarrassment of the dictators whose mission it was to maintain our countries in semifeudal state. But there is more; in our countries, as in those similar to ours, impediments that seemed a part of our nature are being conquered—the ones that made our declaration of national independence simply sentimental statements. As a consequence of the inevitable development to which the societies of all these countries are subject, groups—social classes—have been formed in each and continue to be formed, which still remember well those who served as motivation and support in the North American movement for independence and its subsequent development. These classes, which now feel themselves dulled and curbed by interests foreign to them, can therefore repeat the accusation made in the North American Declaration of Independence against the English king: "He has combined with others to subject us to a jurisdiction foreign to our constitution, and unacknowledged by our laws." These were the words of a nation which rose up against the interests endeavoring to suppress it, words which may now be repeated by many nations in America and other parts of the world which demand equality among men and nations and the right to the pursuit of happiness. These same Western nations—among them the nation that first

75

used the words—are now realizing the importance of the existence of the liberal democratic movement which has now spread to all parts of the earth. This is a fact without any totalitarian implication, although the enemies of liberal democracy have tried to make such a connection in order to justify repressions and new impediments. Latin America, as well as countries elsewhere, marches toward the realization of the kind of world that the most eminent nations pioneered.

Latin America does not find itself alone in this task. Distant countries propose plans which once seemed strange to us but which now remind us of our own. The Far East, mysterious Africa, the exotic Arab world, the countries of the Malay peninsula—all speak to us now in a language that we recognize as common to us all because our problems are the same. We have become conscious of the fact that our own world is not limited to the West; most peoples in the world share the longing to take part in the universal task which until a short time ago seemed to belong exclusively to the West. Many men elsewhere strive for the same principles for which Latin American nations have struggled.

Latin Americans are witnessing the reaction of a whole world against being thrust into a marginal position as a consequence of Western expansion. These other countries now demand rights that exactly coincide with ours as well as obligations that should belong to all men. More than a century and a quarter ago, Hegel, the philosopher of history, noted the marginal character of non-European and non-Western countries. Latin American countries are still marginal. For Hegel, Europe was the only incarnation of the spirit that made history possible. Europe—and the West we might add—was the past of that history of which the

West is the protagonist. It was the past, and therefore had no reason to continue to exist.

And what of our America? Within the Hegelian concept, it was the future, the possibility, but a future and a possibility which, though not yet having achieved being, was purely and simply unreal. And what of Africa? Black Africa, which had given slaves to strengthen European and Western economy in an age in which machines had not yet replaced the hand of man even for the roughest work, had neither past nor future. It was still the ineffable, that which perhaps would be able to achieve being some day but, for the present, could not speak for itself. It was a spirit in its most natural state—a possibility so remote that the outcome remained unpredictable.

Thus Europe, and all the rest of the Western world, has philosophically justified its pre-eminence, its assumed right to dominate the other nations. It dominated some nations because their time had passed; others, because their time had not yet arrived; and the rest because they were not even —nor could they be—historical possibilities. Consequently, our Latin American countries formed a part of the marginal, the unreal world and, for that reason, had no right or reason to oppose what was reality—the progress of civilization on the move.

This situation has changed in our time. Along with others, our countries now resist being shadows or futures without possibilities. They are, rather, countries that are dynamic, alive, current, real, countries that want to be part of a history of all countries and all men which includes them. Thus our countries are placed on the margin of an assumed past, conceded only a future and relegated to the furthest limits of possibility, demanding that which they hold to be their rights as nations among nations with men who know themselves to be part of a community of men.

To be sure, as other philosophers have said, history has always moved toward the West: from Asia to the Middle East, from the Middle East to Greece, from Greece to Rome, from Rome to Western Europe, and from there to the United States. If this movement is to continue, the West now reaches toward the countries that in an earlier age were for Europe part of the Far East. These countries are now looming up more and more as the immediate future of the history that all peoples are going to make. Sukarno of Indonesia was therefore able to say that the nations of Asia are old ones that now experience a rebirth in achieving for themselves independence and freedom.

Although the efforts of Latin America to achieve incorporation in the new world of independence and freedom are much older, it belongs among the regions struggling for these same goals. Putting to one side the different circumstances, habits, and daily customs, we discover in the Asiatic a man like the rest of us—indeed, a man so similar that he seems a replica, our image in a mirror whose depths we had not heretofore probed. Many other peoples have also seemed even further beyond our comprehension: the black men in Africa, even though many of her sons have entered into the flesh and blood of this America, people who are, nevertheless, strange to our understanding, more exotic even than the Asiatics. Countries which still seemed to us to be in a primitive state have, however, filled us with surprise when we learned that they stand for the same principles that we have in the course of our history. Now, in the middle of the twentieth century, they are struggling for the dearest rights of man and the happiness of their people, just as we have been doing since the beginning of the nineteenth century. Black countries no longer form part of a world that we consider primitive but are countries in which problems similar to ours are debated. They now speak the language that we have been using for a century and a half.

Occidental countries themselves have taken account of the fact, which they can interpret only as favorable to themselves, that the language, the arsenal of ideas embraced by these countries, was learned from them or at least taken from them—stolen as Prometheus stole the fire of the gods in order to make it available for man's well-being. In effect, the countries of Africa as well as others utilize Western language and principles. They have made use of the reasons they have learned from the West. Thus the West has been the great teacher of contemporary history, as Greece was of ancient times, although in spite of itself. Countries that have represented for the West the past or the near future are now linked in a present which pertains to all without discrimination in the working out of a future which also must belong to all. The West produced these means, but countries of the rest of the world have had to appropriate them in order to make them their own. In this connection, a Western intellectual, Jean-Paul Sartre, referred to this rebellion, to the actual rebellion of the black nations, which have had to steal the means which permit them to liberate themselves when he said, "The herald of the black soul passed through white schools according to the immutable law which denies any power to the oppressed in order that he may not rob the oppressor himself."[3]

[3] Léopold Sédar-Senghor, ed., *Anthologie de la nouvelle poésie nègre et Malgache de langue française*, précédée de *Orphée Noir* par Jean-Paul Sartre (Paris, 1948), xv.

Means, ideas, words, and dreams come to these countries and to ours from contact with a world which is theirs too. Their sacrifices and the misery and hard labor of their sons have created the world that pertains to all, although some wish to deny that right of common possession. Freedom, sovereignty, democracy, social justice, and many other ideas and ideals have been taken from the arsenal of Western culture by countries which have undertaken the difficult task of applying these to their situations as the Western nations have done.

In speaking about similarities between Latin America and the new world that is being constructed to the west of us on the basis of a past that has just begun to recede into the past, Sukarno said on the occasion of his visit to Mexico:

> I bring greetings from eighty-seven million Indonesians to you. . . . There are many similarities between us; similarities in our problems and also, I believe, in the solutions we search for to these problems.[4]

He had encountered such similarities in the other Latin American countries he had visited. He remarked further:

> Latin America is made up principally of countries still in the revolutionary process. In their political outlook, in their social and economic structure, they have not achieved stability. Many parts of the world have attained a satisfactory stability, but Latin America, like Indonesia and the greater number of Asiatic nations, has not. . . . Wherever I travel I point out that Indonesia is a revolutionary nation, and I always emphasize the fact that there can be no rest for a revolutionary nation. Here, in the countries of Latin America, I feel myself to be among

[4] *Novedades*, May 27, 1959. This quotation and the immediate following are from the same source.

revolutionary countries which as a consequence cannot afford to rest.

There is, however, more, and something that probably surprises us. For a long time Afro-Asiatics have been taking notice of us and learning from our experiences. In our successes and failures they have seen what to emulate and what to avoid. Latin America has not been for them strange or exotic, as they have been for us. Sukarno referred also to the inspiration that the nationalist leaders of his and other countries in Asia have found in our struggles to achieve what has also been their goals—struggles to make their countries modern ones capable of co-operating on a plane of equality in finding solutions for the problems that afflict the world. He added that their leaders and countries, in their liberating and revolutionary struggles, found "a source of inspiration in the struggles of the Latin American countries and in their heroic leaders, Hidalgo and Juárez, San Martín and Bolívar."

What do these new nations of Asia and Africa ask for? The same, I repeat, that we do. Like us, heirs of a very rich culture which they have not renounced, they demand for themselves what we have been demanding from the West. Sukarno stated:

> We demand the right to cure ourselves of the wounds of colonialism and the results of being trampled on. We demand a condition of equality and of equal consideration for our nation and our people in the world of today. Simply, we cannot be second-class citizens.

Has not this been the language of our countries?

We cannot continue being undeveloped countries and, on that account, subordinated to interests foreign to us. Asia and Africa, and along with them Latin America, ask

81

for readjustment of those interests in such a manner that they will be adapted to the new circumstances which the actions of the West have created. The world to which the West gave origin now requires a reconsideration which will take into account the interests of all countries without exception so that all may be accommodated and balanced. Sukarno could not avoid alluding to this urgent necessity when he said with reference to the world that has arisen as a result of Western actions against the rest of the people who inhabit the earth:

> No matter how inflexible the Western world may appear, it will have to find the necessary flexibility to accommodate the new nations of Asia, Africa, and Latin America; that is the responsibility of the older nations. We, the men of the new nations, cannot solve the problem; we can only indicate that it exists and urge its resolution in the interest of the whole world. We can only demand the free and rapid acceptance of new international standards adjustable to the new structure and outlook of the world.

Are We Headed Toward an Era of Solidarity?

VI

THE NATIONALISTIC MOVEMENTS of our countries are far removed from any form of expansionism. The defensive nationalism expressed among us has not been and can never be a barrier in the way of international solidarity, a circumstance not possible with expansionist nationalism. It is easier for men and countries that defend themselves or defend something to reach an accord for common action than it is for those who want something, a something available only to those supposed to be the most competent and capable. Western nationalism achieves a degree of solidarity only in the face of possible mortal danger, but abandons it when the menace disappears; in any event, Western alliances last only during the threatening danger.

Once World War II was over, the ablest of the Western allies began to displace the less able. The United States began doing to its Western allies—England, France, and Belgium—what England had earlier done to Spain's empire in the New World—that is, destroying it in order to impose an empire of its own. We can now discern the development of the problem of the Middle East, which broke out again with the expropriation of the Suez Canal and the Anglo-French intervention in Egypt. The United States then enunciated the famous thesis of the existence of a vacuum in that area which it would have to fill in order to prevent its falling under Soviet influence. France and England had indeed left a vacuum, but only as a consequence of stimulation by the United States in the manner in which it had produced other vacuums in various areas in Africa and Asia. The process was one of displacement of the somewhat anachronistic imperialism of Western Europe in order to establish another imperialism, perhaps more subtle, less in need of forces of occupation—one economic in nature but no less imperialistic. This has resulted in the same economic —and consequently political as well—subordination of Western Europe itself. That is to say, Western solidarity has been relative, for above it has been the specific interests of the allies, with the prize going to the most capable, the most efficient, in accordance with Western doctrine.

In contrast to that rather relative solidarity, a community of interests, impossible among nations that expand by displacing other interests with their own, is beginning to develop among the new nations that have arisen in the world today. These nations lack expansionist aspirations; their attitudes are only defensive. Certain countries having the same cultural origins are beginning to feel this solidarity, as among the Arabs, in spite of the inevitable differences among them that are nothing more than expressions of their inherent characteristics. This solidarity has expanded to include the most uncommitted countries, and was expressed in all its vigor in the conference at Bandung in 1955. Even then Latin American countries had already begun to feel this sort of community of interest among themselves. An even more decided sense of solidarity had already become apparent among all non-Western nations, as I have pointed out.

Great nationalist leaders like Nehru, Sukarno, and Nasser

have often emphasized the need for solidarity among Afro-Asiatics. According to Nehru,

> However different we are from the Chinese and Japanese, or the Indonesians or Arabs, we are, I imagine, more capable of mutual understanding than Europeans or Americans are of comprehending peoples of Asia. Old methods and old habits die with difficulty, and the destiny of Asia is determined by the statesmen of the Western world without their actually taking into account the Asiatic countries directly interested.[1]

The problems of Asia, Nehru went on to say, can be solved only by Asiatics themselves. There are the problems of Korea, Formosa, and the Middle East, regulated according to the interests of the West without considering the point of view of their own people, who should be the most interested in these conflicts. Nehru said with reference to Korea:

> I don't complain, but I wish to emphasize the danger in trying to solve these problems without taking Asia into consideration. They don't do anything but bang their heads against a wall. . . . [On the other hand] we find ourselves in a peculiar position . . . which may permit us, perhaps, to understand better the aspirations of the people of Korea, of China, of Indonesia, or of Indochina. . . . I maintain that, in regard to Asiatic problems, we are in a more favorable situation for understanding and convincing each other than are some Western countries, whose methods, permit me to say with all humility, seem to lack any subtlety.

[1] *Novedades*, December 17, 1956. This quotation and the immediate following are from the same source.

Not possessing any understanding of the Asiatic heart and spirit, they can only fail. This point of view, basic to a genuine solidarity, alien to that resulting from special interests, was effective in the face of Western European aggression against Egypt. It functioned also against the aggression in Lebanon, justified, like that in Korea, by the cold war.

In the discussion of the case of Lebanon before the United Nations, the significance of the intervention of the Latin American nations, expressing a community of interests with its people, is worth noting. On that occasion the Afro-Asiatic as well as the Latin American nations declined to allow Lebanon, and with it the whole of the Levant, to be made into a new Korea for testing new armaments and measuring the power of the opponents in the cold war. As in Korea, the great international rivals found ready pretexts for intervention in support of groups most in accord with them. In 1958, at the request of President Camille Chamoun, who transformed a civil war into part of the cold war, the United States intervened with troops in Lebanon, just as the English had intervened in Jordan at the request of Hussein. Immediately, in the face of that intervention, there came the menace of Russia's sending volunteers reminiscent of the Chinese "volunteers" who in Korea had faced Western forces who had intervened at the request of President Syngman Rhee. When this effort to convert the Levant into a new Korea proved impossible, the United States and the U. S. S. R. each attempted to solve the problem in particular ways which would correspond to its own interests but which were at variance with the interests of the countries suffering internal conflicts.

The solution that had to be accepted was consequently

surprising. The Arab countries themselves, putting aside their differences, agreed that they should be the ones to seek the most suitable settlement for the problems they faced. In their view, it was an internal problem of the Arab nations that only Arabs could and should solve. All the Arab countries represented at the United Nations—those considered pro-Western as well as the nationalistic ones more inclined to the left—were in agreement with this solution. The United States, the U. S. S. R., and other countries too which wanted to intervene in the internal affairs of the countries of the Middle East, had to withdraw their suggestions and accept the only valid proposal—that of the interested countries.

How did the Latin American countries proceed in this situation? From the beginning they acted in accord with the Arab nations in opposing the actual intervention carried out by the United States and threatened by Russia. They maintained the same position which they had upheld against intervention by the United States or any other country—the thesis of nonintervention. Their attitude, manifested as soon as the problem came before the United Nations, surprised the United States, which was accustomed to the unconditional alignment with it, if not of the peoples, at least of many of the governments of Latin America. But Latin America, which had just been in the process of ridding itself of dictatorships made possible by interventionism, was in no mood to align itself in this or any similar case with a point of view which might at some time be the basis for a menace to its own security. Having on various occasions insisted on the principle of nonintervention, the Latin American nations obviously shared the point of view of the Arabs and of the Afro-Asiatic bloc.

Strengthened by its numbers, the Latin American bloc in

the United Nations accepted in principle the proposals which President Eisenhower suggested, but with the addition of the principle of nonintervention even when governments, as in Lebanon and Jordan, called for intervention. Latin America was attempting to obviate the justification of the kind of situations in which they had found themselves many times—that is, the approval and moral sanction before the United Nations which might permit the intervention in one country by another, or by an international organization, at the petition of a government which might consider itself endangered by an internal rebellion and would justify the aggression from outside disguised as help. It had happened that way in Asia and immediately thereafter in America.

Moreover, much of what the United Nations itself had condemned could be thus justified. The intervention of Russia in Hungary might be fully justified because it had been made at the request of Janos Kadar's government, thus transforming what had been a rebellion or civil war into a war between the Hungarian government and so-called foreign agents, in spite of the fact that they were Hungarian workers—in other words, a struggle against capitalist aggression. Chamoun of Lebanon in calling for North American intervention, or Hussein of Jordan in calling on the English, did the same thing, making rebellions of their people appear to be aggressions of Communist imperialism.

Latin America could not fail to take notice of the meaning of the reasons given for these aggressions and interventions presented before the United Nations in the name of peace and the supposed security of the free world or of the socialist world. The histories of Latin American countries were full of that kind of aggression and justification. Acceptance of this thesis of intervention by one power in the affairs of other weaker nations would make it difficult for Latin American countries to continue their revolutions for the purpose of removing the dictatorships and oligarchies which have subjugated them. These illegitimate governments, at the service of foreign interests, would be able to take recourse in the expedients used by Chamoun, Hussein, Rhee, and others in order to solicit the intervention of those foreign interests or that of an international organization to suppress any rebellion of their peoples and to transform civil wars, which could put an end to the power of foreign interests, into international conflicts.

By this means any protests, any reaction, against oppression and dictatorship could be prevented as acts contrary to the security of the free world; indeed, contrary to liberty and democracy and crushed with foreign help, also justified in the name of the security of the free world. And, on the other side, the U. S. S. R. could equally continue justifying its intervention, no matter how brutal, in the area under its influence. In the name of the great values of the free world of the West, violated and disregarded by governments foreign to the peoples who suffer under them, all expectation of the realization of those values would be crushed.

This is not a new problem for our Latin American countries. The problem of the Middle East was not yet resolved, and various dictators and governments alien to their peoples were already demanding—and would continue to demand—interventions to suppress alleged conspiracies against the security of the continent and the free world. According to some news organizations, the grand paladins of liberty and democracy, like the tyrannical Trujillo of Santo Domingo and the heirs of Somoza of Nicaragua, were calling for help and foreign intervention to put down rebellions of the peoples they had suppressed and who had been aroused by the triumphs of others in situations similar to theirs. Such

89

petitions for help were made in the same terms as those of Chamoun, Rhee, and Chaing Kai-shek. Help was requested not only to suppress internal protest but also to put down those who had inspired these rebellions, as in Cuba and Venezuela. Here, as in Korea, Formosa, Lebanon, and Jordan, there was talk of Communist conspiracies, of plots against the security of the continent and against the free world, with appeals for means to suppress them. Our countries once more united, repudiated the new aggression disguised as being in defense of liberty and democracy and sustained the principle of nonintervention.

In favor of intervention in the name of security of the free world and of our continent, there soon appeared such new leaders as Rojas Pinilla, Manuel Odría, Pérez Jiménez, Fulgencio Batista, and Carlos Castillo Armas, soliciting the intervention of foreign forces. There also appeared in Latin America other governments determined to suppress all movements. Thus it was yesterday, and thus it might continue if our countries do not act together.

There is another important aspect of this solidarity among Latin American countries and between them and other countries in a similar situation. Such common action could be a means for preventing the reappearance of illegitimate governments, of dictatorships. The great search now is for solidarity as a means of checking the appearance of new dictatorships not only in Latin America but also in any other part of the world. Thus it might be possible to aid truly free countries in promoting the freedom of others and in preventing new attempts against that freedom.

This laudable objective can be achieved only when the solidarity now emerging becomes a fact, not before—that is, not before our countries are strong enough to control whatever can be utilized for the benefit of the interests which ferment and sustain these dictatorships. Latin Americans have sufficient highly moral grounds to intervene against the enemies of freedom; but we must be careful that such intervention does not offer justification, in turn, for those who suppress freedom in the name of freedom. As long as we do not have the force that solidarity must give us, our right to intervene in support of true freedom can be turned against us. Our history is full of bitter experiences in these matters. In Central America and the Caribbean, filibustering hoisted the banner of liberty in order to destroy democratic and free governments, accusing them of tyranny. This tactic was used in 1954 against the democratically elected government of Guatemala. That government was accused of being an instrument of international communism, and a dictatorship was imposed—by whom nobody knows—on the people. Castillo Armas was presented not only as the defender of continental solidarity but also as a liberator. And was not this same sort of thing said in Trujillo's Santo Domingo of the liberating expeditions which might have freed the people of Venezuela and Cuba of the dictatorships under which they were suffering?

Thus any interventionist position without regard to its defensibility—such as for restraining new acts against the freedom of certain countries or for enabling others to establish it—will be a two-edged sword as long as the solidarity of our countries is not capable of offsetting the force of the great powers which have an interest in these violations of freedom. None of our countries, however democratic or liberal, is safe from the accusation of being a dictatorship. By means of such an accusation, the affected interests, precisely because of that freedom and democracy, may be mobilized to suppress the government in the name—inevitably—of intervention for the sake of freedom. All this

91

will continue to be possible if our countries and their truly legitimate governments do not discover a kind of unity which will restrain intervention alien to their interests made in the very name of the highest values that Latin America longs to achieve.

Our America now possesses an experience that should not be thrown overboard, an experience which, above all, could be valid for countries in other parts of the world that find themselves in a situation similar to ours—that of experiencing many dictatorships and of discovering how these were maintained and how they were eliminated. These dictatorships, in the first place, achieved something that our greatest men of liberty had not been able to achieve—solidarity. But it was a solidarity in crime. Neither barriers nor distance could contain it. It was a solidarity among those who suppressed their countries and pawned their sovereignty. They achieved unity not only with the interests which enjoyed the products of those countries but also among themselves—one dictatorship with another. We saw such unity between Pérez Jiménez of Venezuela and Batista of Cuba, between these and Rojas Pinilla of Colombia, and between all these and Odría of Peru, and between them and Juan Perón of Argentina. That solidarity expressed itself in the same way that the entire wave of dictatorship spread, encouraged not only by the familiar foreign interests but also by the dictatorships already established in the southern part of South America. Everyone knows of the stimulus that the other American dictatorships received once that of Perón in Argentina was secure. All the unity they achieved was among themselves—and all at the service of interests extraneous to America.

It is necessary then to ask ourselves whether unity is possible only through crime. Cannot our countries with a thousand and one similar problems, aside from the great similarity and brotherhood deriving from our cultural heritage, unite in freedom? Are we going to repeat the same old errors—that is, are we going to remain outsiders, once more isolated and exposed to new waves of dictatorships? Shall we again be islands of freedom exposed to tides and cross-currents instead of a continent united in freedom? Cannot the solidarity in freedom of Latin American countries be substituted for the solidarity in crime of the dictators?

It is urgent that we learn the lesson and prevent the return of the trend opposed to freedom. Our countries which in one way or another have maintained their freedom, as well as those which have become free after overcoming obstacles, should initiate a great dialogue to strengthen their ties of friendship, solidarity, and collaboration. Such a dialogue cannot provide serious difficulties among countries of the same cultural origin. Other countries more divided than ours have already sought means to end those divisions, to offset their conflicting interests, and to seek forms of community that will give them strength in the face of their vicissitudes in a world still ruled by the pre-eminence of the strongest. Our strength can come only through unity. Why has not our America been able to do this? Other countries—in the Arab world, in Africa, in Asia, and even in Europe itself—are, as we have seen, able to unite and put aside even racial and religious differences much greater than ours. Why not we?

All those other countries, on joining together, seek an idea which may give them a feeling of unity. We Latin Americans have that idea, a history of that idea, and the means in our history for realizing it. That idea achieved its maximum expression in the concepts of Bolívar. The efforts made by the Iberian world, from the moment it extended

93

its frontiers and created our America to form a single world, were summed up in the thought and the ideals of the Liberator. The efforts of the great Erasmians were directed toward trying to create from Spain a great community in which the best of the inherited past could be assimilated with the best that the future might offer. This dream of Iberian community which might be extended to the whole world, like the Christian empire of which Luis Vives, Alfonso de Valdez, Francisco de Vitoria, and Bartólome de las Casas dreamed, was also the dream of Bolívar for America.

The basis for that solidarity, not only Hispanic but Latin American and universal as well, is found in Bolívar's letter from Jamaica, as well as in many other works of his. He conceived a unity among countries that considered themselves equal and therefore had the same rights and obligations. Bolívar wrote, "I want more than anyone else to see America formed into the greatest nation of the world less by reason of its extent and wealth than by virtue of its freedom and glory."[2] Such a nation would have as a basis for its unity something more than the transient interests and material riches which have motivated the great Western countries of the modern world, something more than merely the aim of dominion by extension of land and territory; instead, its basis would be freedom and glory, values which do not separate but unite those who endeavor to achieve them. The ideal would be a community of nations united for something more than the egoism of modern societies, which aspire at best to achieve a relative equilibrium of interests for fear of losing more than they would gain from the disturbance of that equilibrium, but an equilibrium

[2] "Contestación . . ." *Obras Completas,* 2 vols. (Havana, 1947), I, 159.

which can be broken if the so-called association grows weak and ceases to be a menace.

Worthy heir and father of an old Iberian idea, Bolívar aspired to create a community—not just a society—of men and countries that recognized that they were linked by similar goals without regard to their specific personalities and their no less specific interests. It would not be an association of those who seek only the relative union that serves their special interests. Freedom and glory should be the objectives, not extensive dominion and enrichment at the cost of other men and countries.

Such an ideal community, wanted by the entire world, could be initiated in America, among countries of the same blood, tongue, religion, and origin. "It is a grandiose idea," Bolívar said, "to aspire to consolidate the New World into a single nation with a single bond that ties its parts to the whole since already they have one origin, one tongue, the same customs, one religion."[3] He stated the point of departure for a larger confederation of nations, but one made up of countries which are equal—not one which would simply be the instrument of the strongest group. Bolívar did not exclude any country from such a confederation. But Latin American nations that joined would have to be strong and capable of making themselves respected by other countries however powerful the latter might be. Bolívar had already found that disunity among countries with similar problems and consequently similar solutions made these countries weak and likely to become political domains at the service of those nations that later became great powers.

It would be possible to arrive at a great union which could deal with the great problems of the world only by

[3] *Ibid.*, 172.

starting from the basis of Iberian unity. Then Ibero-America would be able to bend its efforts toward finding the solution of these problems. Thus Bolívar dreamed of the Congress of Panama, not of what might be effective some years later under the dominion of a great power in order to vindicate its external policy and for the purpose of brandishing the solidarity of fear as a weapon in its struggle against another great power antagonistic to it. Bolívar wrote:

> How beautiful it would be for the Isthmus of Panama to be for us what Corinth was for the Greeks! O that some day we may have the good fortune to install there an august congress of representatives of republics, kingdoms, and empires for consultation and discussion about the high interests of peace and war with the nations of the other three-quarters of the world.[4]

✓The Iberian community—or Latin America—could be a point of departure for the creation of a world in which the voice of our countries would be effective and would count decisively in world destiny. More than an association, it would be a community of those having something in common—not a society of those uniting their efforts through fear. This community would aim to achieve or to maintain freedom and other human values no less noble; it would not be merely an association necessary for survival. It would be a great community founded through the free will and sovereignty of countries with a common destiny—not an association of frightened sardines that obey the shark, as Arévalo said, for fear of being devoured by the shark at least or postponing the destiny the shark has indicated for them.

Bolívar wrote of his dream:

[4] *Ibid.*, 294.

96

The homeland of all Americans should be only one, for we are otherwise united. . . . When the triumph of arms completes the work of independence, or when more favorable circumstances permit us closer communications, we will hasten with the most lively interest to initiate on out part the American pact that, forming our republics into a political body, will present America to the world with an aspect of majesty and grandeur without example among the nations of old. If heaven concedes us what we pray for, America could thus be called the queen of nations and the mother of republics.[5]

Unity was essential if the Ibero-American republics were to be respected in a world established for the benefit of the strongest. Bolívar wrote: "Divided we will be weaker, less respected by enemies and neutrals. Union under a single supreme government will provide our strength and will make us formidable before all."[6]

We would be strong, yes, but not in order to exploit and dominate the weaker but, instead, in order to collaborate as equals in the construction of the future of a world that will relate to all men and all countries. Without accompanying strength, Latin American collaboration would mean only subordination, as Bolívar understood when he said: "Once the pact is made with the strong, the obligation of the weak is permanent. Everything considered, we shall have tutors in youth, masters in maturity."[7] To make pacts with those who are strong without also being strong is to prepare for subordination. For that reason Bolívar feared the union with England, which, even though it could serve Latin America well because England was strong, could also be

[5] Bolívar to Juan Martín de Pueyrredón, 1818, *ibid.*, 294.
[6] Bolívar to Santiago Mariño, December 16, 1813, *ibid.*, 81.
[7] Bolívar to Bernardo Monteagudo, August 5, 1823, *ibid.*, 791.

97

the beginning of a new subordination. All the advantages, Bolívar wrote,

> do not dissipate the fears that the powerful nation may in the future be sovereign of the councils and decisions of the assembly, that its voice may be the most penetrating, and that its will and its interests may be the soul of the confederation, that no one would dare to displease it for fear of coming up against an irresistible enemy. In my opinion this is the major danger in the association of one such nation with others that are weak.[8]

In our own time, it would be necessary only to replace the name of England with that of the nation which has taken its place in that absurd association between the strong and the weak. All this, however, provides a point of departure for the achievement of a more universal community in which the strong would not menace the weak inasmuch as all would be strong.

Can we realize this dream now that distances have been shortened, now that the interests of all—both the strong and the weak—are closely linked? Can all the Latin American countries create a community that will permit them to enter into discussions and to balance interests with their powerful neighbor of the north as equal with equal in the search for solutions of problems of both our continents? Will the Latin American community, on its part, be effective in finding solutions for all world problems, with its efforts joined by that of other groups, united not by reason of tongue, religion, or culture but by the situation resulting from the common impact of Western influence? Will the Latin American community, united with other groups

[8] Bolívar, in draft of letter to José Rafael Revenga, February 17, 1826.

formed for the same reasons—the Arabs, the Africans, and the Asiatics—have sufficient weight to form another even more powerful group and thus be able to balance their interests with those of the primary powers?

Bolívar held that a community of our countries could be the basis for a wider community that could be extended to the countries of Asia and Africa, in order to make them free and to destroy the yokes that Europe—that is, the Western world—had established over them, in order to form, with all those countries and of course with the others that make up the earth, a new and powerful union that would be comparable only to the one that Iberia dreamed of expanding throughout the world in order to create a great united Christian world in which all men could be equal. "In the march of centuries," said Bolívar, "it might, perhaps, be possible to find only one nation covering the entire earth."[9]

[9] "Un pensamiento sobre el Congreso de Panamá," 1826, *ibid.*, II, 1215.

Index